VENTURE CAPITAL MINDSET

Become the candidate that every venture capital firm would like to hire

Renata George

To my best friends:

My Son, who learns fast and has become my true business partner.

My Mother, who allowed me to live the life I wanted.

My Man, who brings out the best in me.

CONTENTS

CHAPTER 5

INTRODUCTION

There are dozens of books and articles available, that teach readers how to get into venture capital. But have you ever actually heard of anyone, who managed to *break* into this industry, crediting a book for helping them to achieve that?

If you've been trying to become a venture investor, or even just trying to find a job in venture capital, but haven't made it, then you know better than anyone how hard it is. All of those books and articles clearly haven't helped. "Breaking" implies that one was lucky enough to unexpectedly become a venture investor. NO book can ever teach you how to be lucky!

So then… why are you holding yet another book about venture capital careers?

A couple of years ago, I was trying to hire an associate for our small corporate venture investing team. I had done the candidate search, the selection, the interviewing and the vetting myself. Hundreds of resumes and dozens of interviews showed me one major pattern: so many applicants have confused being hired by a venture capital firm, with becoming a venture investor. To them, an employment agreement seemed like they were halfway to becoming the next John Doerr, while it actually means very little, if anything at all. Even those who wanted to learn the art of venture investing, didn't see their career path clearly, so they wanted to work for a VC firm, simply for the sake of working for a VC firm.

It takes at least nine years to become a licensed doctor in the United States. Few people actually realize that becoming a professional venture investor is a similarly long and arduous process, which can easily take nine years for the first profitable exit to happen. However, unlike in the medical profession, one can call oneself an investor from the first day they are hired. For many aspiring venture investors, this is an important achievement, while it really is just the very beginning of a big challenge.

It was precisely because of this misconception, that too many of the applicants I met didn't put their skin in the game, and they lacked the commitment I was looking for. I could teach anyone everything I know about venture capital, so I wasn't concerned about their knowledge and skills, but their endgame—or the absence thereof—mattered a lot to me.

Choosing to work in venture investing should be a calling, like becoming a doctor: you need to know what it is you want, why you want to *get* into the venture capital industry, and most importantly, how to *stay* there long enough to achieve the true success.

When I graduated from high school, I forced myself to follow my family's medical career path and decided to study at a medical school. I use the word "forced" because I never saw myself as a doctor, despite there being several generations of medical practitioners in my family. When my father passed away, I read that as a sign that I should at least try to become one. My parents and grandparents were all very respected doctors, so I wouldn't have had to worry about graduating from medical school with honor. Yet, after two years of theoretical studies and passing all my tests flawlessly, I quit. After my first practical class, I finally admitted to myself that I would never enjoy medical practice. On the same day, and with no parental consent, I transferred to the "Financial Management of a Medical Organization" faculty.

I have worked with business enterprises and investments for 15 years since then, having raised my first fund and become a managing partner six years after graduating from university. I was subsequently hired by a foreign venture capital firm to help them make their way to the United States. Oh, and during this entire process, I had to deal with being an immigrant in the US.

Although I never thought I would end up in venture capital, when I decided to choose my own career, somehow all of the opportunities I could only have wished for presented themselves thereafter, and I took them with confidence, because I knew what I wanted. That is so much better than chasing each and every new job posting and begging for someone to hire you, don't you think?

Thousands of people keep applying for venture capital jobs around the world, but very few of them actually get hired. When I realized how many people are chasing venture capital as merely an employment opportunity instead of their true calling, I decided to put together everything I have done in my career, and to align it with the expectations of mature venture capitalists for their team members. I talked to dozens of acting venture investors, then deconstructed my past efforts, looked at each bit carefully, improved them, and then assembled them in a structured manual. I started mentoring young investment professionals, and then redesigned my mentoring practice into a coaching program. Today, I am presenting this book to you because I want to make my coaching available and accessible to even more young investment professionals and aspiring investors everywhere—not only in the United States. I want you to know more about venture capital than I did when I started investing.

How this book is different

Venture capitalists are well known for codifying their answers about investing practices, because nobody wants to share their "secret sauce". You can't blame them—competition for the next unicorns and FOMO ("fear of missing out") are very high! However, this codification has made venture investing practices look like sacred knowledge, and passing the skill from one venture investor to another almost seems like the transfer of an ancient family's secret for tea brewing through generations. As such, the knowledge barrier that people encounter when trying to enter the venture capital industry is rather formidable, because very few belong to this family and have access to "the master". Existing offline venture capital educational programs are pretty short, because, traditionally, only common knowledge is shared—and expensive nonetheless. The price tag for longer programs has six digits before the comma!

In fact—and I sense that many of my colleagues are upset with me for saying this—venture investing has become a discipline for, I'd say, a good 80% of the practice. The rest belongs to the famous gut feeling—which we'll talk about in this book—and to luck. Whatever can be taught, you are able to find and easily learn at your own pace, from a few well-structured, comprehensive educational programs, such as that offered by www.vc.academy. The rest needs to be practiced, but that would be impossible without a strong foundation of knowledge.

There's no chance that a single book can provide such a foundation for you, so don't buy marketing slogans—you'll need to read a good couple of dozen books. That is why this book won't be teaching you VC slang, or explaining deal-making documents, but it will point you to a list of the best resources where you can learn all that. The book will also not try to convince you, yet again, about how important networking is, but give you some guidance on building relationships with decision-makers. Nor will it tire you with biographical interviews—that is what Google is for.

The main goal of this book is to make you a desirable candidate for potential employers among VC firms, by helping you with building your investor profile and developing your venture capital mindset.

Getting into venture capital is not about a job... it is about YOU. Yes, the book covers the process of finding a VC job, however, that won't be just any VC job—it will be the right VC job for *you*.

Aside from teaching you how to find such a job, the book will also set you up for picking winners by using the different strategies, models, and tools that, when used together, will change the way you possibly view venture capital.

In order to maximize and secure your future, you will, in turn, need to understand your place in the venture capital world. At the end of the day, *breaking* into venture capital is not just about adding the word "investor" to your Twitter bio. It's about becoming a venture investor to your core, whether you end up at a VC firm or on your own as an angel investor (yes, you'll become more conscious about your career choices too).

This book will provide you with the tools you will need, and the instructions for using them. It is up to you to feel them out, try and improve them for yourself, and add whatever else might be needed, because there is no one universal recipe for becoming a venture investor.

During the course of this book, I will be encouraging you to apply these tools and instructions immediately after you have learned them. Some of them will work for you only sometimes, and some will work better than others.

Think of this book as sport lessons—pick any sport of your choice, whether it's tennis or golf. To become a good player you need to practice. Unless you practice, the tools that I give you will remain words on paper. You need to embed the tools in your daily routine and make them work for you, in order to own them. This is as true for sport as it is for venture capital. After all, successful venture investors are made—not born.

Learning fast, staying relevant, evaluating risks, making decisions, etc.—these and a bunch of other skills are critical for a venture investing, as they are for other situations in life. That is why venture capital is so much more than a discipline and an investing practice—it's a mindset.

With practice, you will internalize the tools described in this book, and they will become habits. They will become second nature to you—as much a part of you as your personality. You will start applying them to virtually every meaningful event in your life, at which point you will realize that you've succeeded in cultivating that venture capital mindset.

Feel free to reach me out at any point through www.renata.vc, to let me know how you are doing. I'm an educator at heart and deeply curious about how my students advance. Although we won't have the luxury of personal coaching for all of you, I promise to respond to every person's first email. This book is intended to establish a dialogue with everyone with an emerging venture investor inside them.

How This Book Works

"Venture Capital Mindset" is my attempt to create a book version of my coaching program, which would be impossible to fit in just one title. That is why I decided to have a very strict focus for the first edition. However, there are so many things that I wish I could explain, and so many additional resources I'd like to direct my readers to, that the tree structure of the book became the best solution.

1. The goal of this book is to make you a desirable candidate for a VC job. Every chapter covers one major subject, bringing you closer to this goal. This is the trunk and branches of the tree.
2. At the end of each chapter you will find the assignments that my coachees usually get. I'll be thrilled if you decide to work on these assignments yourself too!
3. All the templates that we use in the coaching program will be available to the readers of this book on my website www.renata.vc in the dedicated section.
4. As a bonus, I also include my reply to your *first* email with any of your questions. I can't promise that I will be able to carry on a dialogue with each of you after my response, although I will try to give you as much feedback as possible.
5. All images used in the book, links to quoted sources, and people I mention, as well as other books that I refer to, and explanations that I avoided including as footnotes, are also available in the relevant section on my website.

6. Because some of the data I've used in the book can become outdated, I'll keep adding relevant updates where possible (for example, studies or market statistics)—all stored on the website.

7. I have so much more to share that this book cannot fit in, so I will be collecting material that is relevant to building a career in venture capital and developing a venture capital mindset, which will be the stems, leaves, and fruits of the tree. I usually distribute such material by email—feel free to subscribe to my updates on www.renata.vc and receive them as soon as they become available.

The access to the additional materials on my website is password-protected. You will find the password at the end of Chapter 1—Assignment 1.

CHAPTER 1

ENTERING FORT KNOX

Do You Think Like An Investor?

"Think like a VC" is probably the most common advice given to entrepreneurs and aspiring investors. When you stumble upon it in yet another article about breaking into venture capital, it seems absolutely legit—until you read further. What does it mean to think like a VC? Some of these advisors keep praising the venture capital mindset, but don't really clarify what it is and how it works. Instead, you read about the legal terms used in venture investing, or you just circle around other codified advice—"think big".

Although all of these things do indeed have a place in a venture capitalist's mind, they are not <u>how</u> an investor thinks, but rather <u>what</u> they think. The "what" of a venture investor's mindset is simple to learn and understand. It is "how" this mindset works, that remains uncovered.

There may be several reasons for that. For example, the advice "think like a VC" is most often given to encourage listeners to learn specific terms, so that they can speak the same language with potential investors, understand what metrics matter to them, and realize that there is nothing personal in their investment decisions. That may be enough for a first-time founder, but this advice doesn't work for those who want to build a venture investing career.

Another reason is that thinking in a particular way comes so naturally to experienced venture investors and seems so obvious, that it's quite difficult for them to explain it in simple words. After all, the "curse of knowledge" isn't selective and happens to VCs too.

Finally, as I've mentioned before, very few people are comfortable sharing their "secret sauce"—their unique ingredient for making millions—with anyone but their apprentices, which is understandable.

Where does this leave us? In a highly competitive talent market where VC firms are looking to hire prodigies who are supposed to possess almost all of the skills and competencies of a partner-level investment professional (don't take my word for it—go to www.vc.academy and read the requirements for an analyst in one of the top-tier VC funds).

This book is an attempt to explain the *how* of a venture investor's thinking and apply it to your job search early on.

Although the book will serve as a step-by-step guide for preparing yourself for a VC job, *how* venture investors think is the core of this book. Not only will I try to explain it to you, but we will also be applying it to different situations. You will be able to see venture investors' decision-making models when it comes to assessing companies, investing in them, and hiring team members. Finally, not to distract you from the main purpose of this book, I'll keep all the explanations as short as possible, and maybe write an extension to the book at a later date. Let's get to it already!

Venture capital as an industry and practice, is very unstructured on different levels, and for different reasons. There are no textbooks available that encompass the entire venture investing practice, as I've mentioned before. The title nomenclature of venture firms is very fluid, and the game rules are constantly changing. So how do we create some structure out of this chaos?

What I want you to do now, is to close this book and take a long and hard look at its cover. What do you see on it? Do you see a lamp or a bulb? Do you see a real device or its model?

Any object that might be on this book's cover is absolutely irrelevant. What I wanted to show you, is a *system*.

There are three main components in any system: the *elements*, their *interconnections*, and their *functions or purpose*. In the case of this cover, you will see a bulb, and other different parts of the lamp, as a construction. You can easily explain how they are interconnected, and most of you will be able to explain why they are connected in this particular way, using your school knowledge of elementary physics.

We can then discuss the fact that the construction might have been more modern and convenient for a user. We might also predict that the lamp's nuts and bolts may loosen over time due to flaws in its engineering. We could even argue that the design matters.

We would all agree that the bulb alone is not quite usable, that the lamp costs more than the bulb alone, and that a well-designed lamp would cost more than this one. We could continue discussing the aspects of the lamp indefinitely, but essentially we are still talking about a lamp—its *elements*, *interconnections*, and their *functions*, and the fact that it is still a *system*.

When evaluating a startup, an investor will view it from several very different perspectives. In the first place, a startup is a system of its own, with its product and all other relevant elements interconnected with each other, all carrying out specific functions or having certain purposes. Think about an early-stage company with a small team, where each member plays several roles at once due to limited resources. It's really easy to imagine this system as our lamp from the cover, where the bulb is the idea, which might either shine brightly or fall and get broken, depending on the rest of elements.

When this startup is then put in the context of the market that it targets, it becomes an element of a larger system, interacting with dozens or even hundreds of other elements. As a result of this interaction, each element—including the startup itself—can change, affecting the entire system, the interconnections between the elements, and the elements themselves.

The next level is embedding our imaginary startup in a venture fund's portfolio, because a venture fund is also a system, and how any other investment opportunity affects the entire portfolio, matters a great deal to a professional venture investor. The way that investors and their own networks contribute to a startup's success is also an important component: will they be able to help the company grow and lead it to a lucrative exit? This is yet another layer of interconnections that may bring change to this system and to the startup, as one of its elements.

Since we've defined that a venture fund is a system, its team members are clearly also elements. Therefore, when you're applying for a job at a venture fund, you need to understand where you will fall as an element in this system. If Sequoia Capital doesn't hire you because you don't have enough experience, it doesn't mean that you have nothing to offer to another venture fund. Each system is different, so you need to find the right fit for you and become a critical element with a purpose and function that provides a positive change to the fund.

When changes occur in a system in a consistent pattern, a feedback loop is created. For example, if you implement certain activities that are described in the book, but none of your job applications have received a response, it only means that you need to change something in your activities. Finding a pattern in the system helps you to control existing behaviors and to create new ones. For instance, you may want to stop sending your resume out blindly, and establish more personal connections in order to pitch yourself to VCs, face to face.

Although, this may seem just like any other common advice, it's not universal either. If a top-level investment professional decides to change their employer, not every personal pitch may be good for him or her. The behavior and feedback loops in this case, will be different.

This is a very short introduction into system thinking. It's an exciting subject, which could easily switch your attention from the goal of finding your place in venture capital, so let's stop here. Bit by bit, we'll be learning more about the systems so that you can apply this approach to your job search.

System thinking as a discipline is very new and, as every new concept, may be sometimes argued. System thinking as a framework of the venture capital mindset is therefore new as well, so I am prepared to debate about this subject with some of my colleagues. I have done my research, however, and found out that many venture investors would rather agree with me — they have been describing something similar, but just called it differently.

For example, Semil Shah, the founder of Haystack and venture partner at Lightspeed Venture Partners, thinks this way: "My belief is that in the VC game, having "context" means possessing the following: You have a network; you hold a point of view on a few topics that matter to you; that other people seek you out for help and advice; you have some understanding as to how the ecosystem's participants — the founders, the early employees, the "joiners," the operators, the angels, the investors, and the press — interact in the game. I believe if you show up in VC without these points of context, you won't be as effective or be able to compete."

Semil is talking about "the ecosystem's participants" and interactions between them "in the game" — which is nothing else but a system.

There are also some VCs who already use "system" as a term talking about venture capital: "Venture is probabilistic. Because it's not a linear, predictable path into the industry, you'll need to take a longer-term systems view. Give yourself a couple years to do this, and be intentional about it." — says Brendan Baker, former for Greylock.

Throughout the book, you will see examples of system thinking as applied to venture investing, and how it is one of the core components of the venture capital mindset. However, you can see right now that system thinking is important in venture capital not only for investing purposes, but for finding a job as well. So let's take it slow and with this sketch in your head, let's start building your mindset.

Have Your Skin In The Game!

Let me break this down for you: venture investing is about paying money for something with an expectation of returns that are not guaranteed. If you want to become a venture investor, you'd better start doing exactly that, right now. It doesn't matter whether you end up working for a venture firm, or become an individual angel investor, or even whether you'll be investing crypto money as a true new generation investor. As long as you deliberately exchange money for something that can potentially provide a return, or better yet, multiply the invested amount, despite there being a good chance of losing it all, you are making a risky investment. What you call yourself really does not matter, at the end of the day, because this is generally what venture investing is.

It's unlikely that someone would entrust their money to a person who hasn't risked his or her own cash in certain roles. To call yourself a venture investor at any stage of your career, you need to truly have your skin in the game, so what will count in that regard?

Clearly, if you have invested individually as an angel investor, you already have a good start. Even if none of your investments have made a successful exit yet, nothing positions you better as an investor, than your personal investment portfolio.

This is, however, not the only way to prove that you have your skin in the game—you can approach it from the opposite side. Investing your cash in your own startup is also a commitment, even if your venture doesn't turn out to be a success at all. As a matter of fact, the more mistakes you make as an entrepreneur, the more you have to share with your future investees. Many venture investors have also been entrepreneurs themselves, but only a few of them have been truly successful.

Finally, if you don't have that much money with which to start your own company or to invest in others, invest in yourself. You need to show your employer, or partners—or even your investees for that matter—that you have something to put on the table. If that "something" is not experience, then at least let it be your knowledge. There are a lot of other candidates who will be competing with you for both a job at a VC firm, and a promising startup to invest in, so you will have to present all the superpowers you have.

You should always approach learning wisely, though. The most popular learning path that people take, is to start with MBA, which actually has little to do with the startup world. Another way is to bury yourself online, reading all of the available publications out there. An enormous amount of unstructured information is never going to be helpful, as opposed to a reasonable amount of well-structured information. Luckily, there are enough sources of quality content to provide you with a good foundation and enable you to harvest your knowledge further. Most of these sources are not free, but hey, this is what I am talking about: have your skin in the game—start investing! Investing in yourself, by the way, is probably the least risky kind of investment there is. Never regret spending money on education, even if you eventually change your mind and never become a venture investor. Most of the lessons and concepts you'll learn will be truly helpful in life.

As you can see, regardless of which path you choose, you really need to get comfortable with bearing the risk of investing with the probability of little or no pay-off.

Now that we have that goal in sight, let's build our way straight up to it.

Meet Venture Capital's Competitors

Before we can hope to navigate the venture investing arena, let's draw a map so that we can understand where venture capital is placed. Firstly, I assume that your ultimate goal is to become a partner, or even a general partner of a venture fund, which means that you will need to raise money from limited partners—institutional investors, corporations, and wealthy families and individuals. Secondly, you need to know whose money is at risk and why they have agreed to that.

When raising money for a venture fund, general partners compete not only with other funds, but more so with other asset classes. It is essential to understand LPs' values, drivers, and the investment mixes of their investment strategies, in order to compete and become more attractive than other assets. So let's meet the competitors of venture capital.

In investing speak, anything that can be converted into cash, is an asset, i.e. the total resources of a person or business, and this includes a person's knowledge, skills, and expertise. I strongly encourage you to think this way from now on. However, for the purpose of this section, let's focus on investment assets only.

Professional investors—like Warren Buffet—invest in different kinds of assets in order to diversify their portfolio (collection of investment assets) for better returns. According to Fidelity Investments, the world's fourth largest multinational financial services corporation, **building a diversified portfolio means betting on assets whose returns have not historically moved in the same direction, and to the same degree, but ideally, move in opposite directions.** For example, if the value of the shares of public corporations is falling, the price of gold, as an asset, will be stable or bulging up. This way, even if a portion of the portfolio is declining, the rest of it is hopefully growing. Thus, some assets that are gaining in value can potentially compensate for other assets that are losing value, thereby keeping the overall portfolio performance positive.

Assets with similar characteristics, market behavior, and that comply with the same laws and regulations, are grouped together in what are called "asset classes".

The main characteristic of any asset is its liquidity, or the ease and speed at which one can buy or sell this asset for its market price. The most liquid asset is obviously cash—you can purchase it immediately or spend it on purchasing other assets. Public equities or stocks, bonds, fixed-income securities, marketable securities, and commodities are the other asset classes that are most liquid. These classes are preferred by most investors, and that is why they are called "traditional assets".

Though traditional asset classes are relatively stable, they can still lose a lot of value. For example, the market capitalizations of 500 large American companies are measured by a special index called the S&P 500, and these fell by as much as 43.84% in 1931 and 36.55% in 2008. The arithmetic average annual return on the S&P

500 in the period 2007-2016, is 8.65%, which after being adjusted to inflation, brings us to a conservative 6-7%. This level of annual return is the average of what any investor would hope for. In comparison, the average bank interest rate on a savings account, is barely 1%.

"The economy, as measured by gross domestic product, can be expected to grow at an annual rate of about 3% over the long term, and inflation of 2% would push nominal GDP growth to 5%. Stocks will probably rise at about that rate and dividend payments will boost total returns to 6-7%".

Warren Buffett, an American business magnate, investor, and philanthropist, a chairman and CEO of Berkshire Hathaway

To reduce the risks of investing in liquid, yet sensitive assets, investors balance their portfolios by investing in other types of assets that typically include one or more of the following attributes: long-term, high-risk, or illiquid investments associated with higher returns; a low correlation with traditional assets; inflation-hedging benefits; and scalability (the ability to absorb large investment sums). Such assets are called "alternative" due to how different they are to traditional assets. The alternative category encompasses a wide range of asset classes, including real estate and infrastructure funds, secondary funds, and private debt funds, as well as private equity buyouts, hedge funds, and venture capital. The last three have accounted for the vast majority of the capital allocated to alternatives (also often referred to as "alternative investments"). This is what we'll focus on.

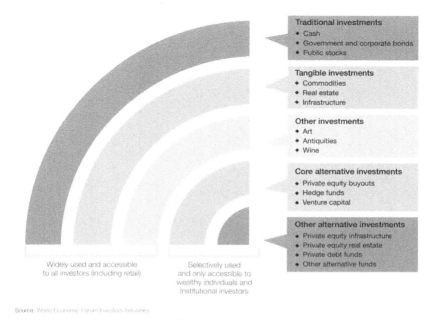

Image 1.1. Overview of different types of investments. Source:
World Economic Forum Investors Industries

By calling an alternative investment 'illiquid', investors mainly mean that it may take more time to find a buyer for this asset when it needs to be converted into cash, thus, an asset's illiquidity does not speak to its return potential. Even during crisis times, history shows us that alternatives have not typically fallen as far as stocks, thereby providing a cushion for investors. Aside from reacting to market changes differently, venture capital as an alternative investment, can provide higher rates of returns due to the rapid value growth of startup companies within a certain period of time. On the graph below, you can see that realized multiples from S&P 500 returns are pretty stable, albeit very conservative, though venture capital investments can provide returns twice as high during better times.

Image 1.2. US venture capital market VS cash-matched S&P 500 total returns. Source: Dow Jones VentureSource

What is the return on invested capital?

Investors put money to work for a certain period of time—it may only be for one year, but typically, we are talking about several years for each investment. If you put $100,000 in a bank with a 1% annual interest rate, you will earn $1,000 after a year, and $5,101 after 5 years. Your return will be 1.01x and 1.05x respectively. As you can see, even a seemingly insignificant return of 1.1x is more attractive than the return on a bank deposit. So when it comes to possible returns of 2x and higher on risky investments such as venture capital, investors get very excited.

Historically, the alternative asset class, as a whole, was able to deliver on investors' expectations, with returns averaging as high as 2x during the dotcom boom. However, following the dotcom crash, returns hovered around 1x for nearly a decade and only in the late 2000s returned to the 1.1x–1.5x range.

Greater returns come with greater risk, and venture capital has the greatest risk among all the asset classes in which institutions invest. Therefore, despite the attractive opportunities and steady interest in venture capital from institutional investors, it still remains an alternative asset class, and tends to be a very small portion of the portfolios of most institutional asset managers.

For example, according to recent data, the average allocation to private equity by US public pension funds, which collectively manage US$3.6 trillion, is only 7%. The largest fund in the US, the California Public Employees' Retirement System, allocated only about 8% of its US$357 billion worth of assets under management, to private equity in general.

Now you know that despite an impressive amount of money being available to venture capital, the competition for it is high.

What Do 'PE' And 'VC' Actually Mean?

Because venture capital, as an investment strategy, falls under the umbrella of private equity as a term, every other day, you may hear these two terms used interchangeably. However, all private equity investment strategies are quite different when compared to each other, and oftentimes, it is important to distinguish venture capital from private equity capital—whether it's growth capital or buyouts—as they may be comparatively opposite approaches.

Out of all private equity investment strategies, growth capital is the closest investment approach to venture capital, which nevertheless still differs substantially, due to the stage at which investors back the companies. As we've figured out, venture capital, by definition, can be invested in very early stage companies with no proven business model. Growth capital, on the other hand, comes into play at later stages when a company has already achieved certain stability.

The line between these two investment strategies gets blurrier and blurrier, due to the following trends: (a) venture funds need to participate in late (growth) investment rounds to save or increase their share in a company (which they may or may not be able to do, depending on the fund's size and investment model), and (b) large venture funds have so much capital that they focus on later stage investing in order to deploy it. Keeping this in mind, here are several key distinctions between growth capital and venture capital:

VENTURE CAPITAL	GROWTH EQUITY
Invest in early stage operating companies with unproven business models	Invest in mature operating companies with proven business models
Invest in multiple early stage companies within an industry/sector	Invest in the (perceived) market leader within an industry/sector
Investment theses underwritten on substantial revenue growth projections	Investment theses underwritten on defined plan to achieve profitability potential
Invest in companies with undefined future capital requirements	Limited or no future capital requirements to achieve profitability potential

Image 1.3. Comparison of VC to growth equity. Source: PE HUB

However, in everyday life, when "private equity" is used as opposed to "venture capital" as a term, the conversation may also refer to "private equity buyouts (PE)", with 'buyout' being the keyword, but often omitted. Buyouts are very different from growth capital and way too far from venture capital—here is how:

CONTROL BUYOUTS	GROWTH EQUITY
Invest in a controlling (or exclusive) equity position	Invest in a minority equity position
Invest in highly profitable operating companies with consistent free cash flow	Invest in operating companies with limited or no free cash flow
Often employ debt financing to leverage the investment	Invest in operating companies with minimal or no funded debt
Invest at point where revenue and profitability are projected to grow steadily	Invest at inflection point where growth capital can fuel substantial revenue and profitability growth

Image 1.4. Comparison of growth equity to private equity buyouts. Source: PE HUB

Private equity, in the strictest sense, defines capital invested in private companies, which either have never been public, or were delisted from a stock exchange due to a buyout. In this case, the buyout happens with the participation of private equity capital. Historically, investment firms that primarily focus on buyouts and boosting later-stage companies with growth capital toward IPOs or other types of exits in the short term, are called PE firms/investors. Other investment firms that fund companies all the way from early to later stages, focusing more on their long-term growth, are called VC firms/investors. As you can see, "private equity" and "venture capital" are not exactly interchangeable, so be aware of this distinction hereafter.

Even though there are some similarities in the way PE and VC firms operate, these similarities are mainly superficial. However, some firms can invest in both PE and VC, making the line between them really blurry. Aside from the semantic imperfection between 'PE' and 'VC' as widely used terms, there is also a philosophical distinction between them. Once you understand it, you can also understand why Wall Street investment bankers sometimes make terrible venture capitalists, and vice versa.

Generally speaking, private equity and venture capital are two distinguishable types of capital, targeting different categories of investments, harvesting them differently, and even being recognized as different alternative asset classes when it comes to signing checks.

Let's consider what private equity and venture capital have in common. Firms of both types:

- Raise capital from outside investors, called limited partners;
- Invest that capital in private companies or companies that become private and attempt to sell those investments at higher prices in the future;
- Are related to an alternative asset class due to lower liquidity than some other classes;
- Utilize legal contracts of the same structure;
- Work with the same financial terminology;
- Exit investments in the same way.

Last, but not least, both types of capital are in the business of buying low and selling high; however, they come at this challenge from fundamentally different directions.

	Private Equity (Growth or Buyouts)	Venture Capital
Environment	Control	Chaos
Medium	Numbers	Human Beings
Primary Hard Tool	Buying and selling stock	Buying and selling stock
Primary Soft Tool	Operational Efficiency	Human Motivation
Primary Lever	Optimized Structure	Disruptive Innovation
Primary Investment Trigger	Underutilized Assets	Team
Industry Focus	Any industry	Certain favorites
Equity Share	Majority stake (controlling)	Minority stake
Deal Size	Larger (due to larger stakes)	From small to large
Investment Structure	Equity and debt	Equity
Stage of business	Mature companies	From seed to growth
Risk tolerance	Low	High
Operational Focus	Deep operational involvement	Low operational involvement
Economic Philosophy	Neoclassical Economics	Innovation Ecosystems ("Rainforests")
Assumption	Rational Actors	Irrational Actors
Role of Probability	Precision	Serendipity
Model	Deming/TQM, Six Sigma	Silicon Valley
Parallels	Classical music, Fine arts, Farms, Assembly lines	Jazz, Street art, Rainforests, Design thinking
Direction of Value Creation	Top-down	Bottom-up

Image 1.5. Comparison of VC and growth capital/buyouts philosophies. Built on the matrix suggested by Victor W. Hwang

The direction of value creation is the very philosophy that sets PE and VC apart. PE usually starts with existing but under-optimized businesses, while VC often starts with nothing but a "crazy idea". Private equity financing is directed at existing companies, their existing products, and cash flows, therefore with the existing value. The goal of such deals is to turn the current value into a higher value, even if a company is one step away from bankruptcy. Venture capital, on the other hand, tends to back more or less early-stage businesses that haven't become profitable, and attempts to bring non-existing value to the same heights.

> *"I consider private equity and venture capital as opposites. In private equity, you start with the numbers, and then you try to fit everything into the numbers. In venture capital, you start with people, and then you try to figure out what numbers you can make."*
> *Mark Kachur, former CEO of CUNO,*
> *a company that was acquired for over a billion dollars.*

These two mindsets are fundamentally different, implementing polar opposite methods of value generation: bottom-up creation (VC) versus top-down optimization (PE). Nevertheless, they meet in the middle and merge organically to achieve their common purpose: a successful exit.

Does private equity growth capital perform better than venture capital deals? Generally, the 5-year annual returns are pretty similar (see benchmarks below) varying in the range of 15-17%

depending on the stage focus. Although these two types of capital both belong to an alternative asset class, they offer investors different levels of risk with comparable rates of returns.

U.S. Venture Capital Index and Selected Benchmark Statistics

Data as of December 31, 2014

U.S. Venture Capital Fund Index Summary: End-to-End Pooled Return
Net to Limited Partners

Index	1-Quarter	1-Year	3-Year	5-Year	10-Year	15-Year	20-Year	25-Year	30-Year
Cambridge Associates LLC U.S. Venture Capital Index®	9.88	21.49	18.04	16.07	10.28	4.84	35.44	22.11	17.67
U.S. Venture Capital - Early Stage Index[1]	10.93	23.09	19.25	16.83	9.81	4.47	56.67	29.41	21.29
U.S. Venture Capital - Late & Expansion Stage Index[1]	4.63	8.87	14.21	16.57	12.80	6.17	11.27	13.15	12.60
U.S. Venture Capital - Multi-Stage Index[1]	9.75	22.99	17.42	14.81	10.33	5.07	13.81	13.33	12.25
Barclays Government/Credit Bond Index	1.82	6.01	2.76	4.69	4.70	5.79	6.24	6.53	7.43
Dow Jones Industrial Average Index	5.20	10.04	16.29	14.22	7.91	5.44	10.48	10.43	12.36
Dow Jones U.S. Small Cap Index	8.46	8.39	20.36	16.38	9.16	8.94	11.31	NA	NA
Dow Jones U.S. TopCap Index	4.86	13.24	18.56	15.54	8.00	4.44	9.89	NA	NA
Nasdaq Composite Index*	5.40	13.40	22.05	15.85	8.09	1.02	9.64	9.83	10.34
Russell 1000® Index	4.88	13.24	20.62	15.64	7.96	4.62	10.04	9.82	11.40
Russell 2000® Index	9.73	4.89	19.21	15.55	7.77	7.38	9.63	9.75	10.27
S&P 500 Index	4.93	13.69	20.41	15.45	7.67	4.24	9.85	9.62	11.33
Wilshire 5000 Total Market Index	5.25	12.71	20.29	15.54	7.99	4.75	9.93	9.71	11.22

Image 1.6. US Venture capital index and selected benchmark statistics. Source: Cambridge Associates

Private Equity Performance – Benchmarks
(as of December 31, 2014)

Private Equity Benchmark Returns (Horizon IRR)	1-Year	3-Year	5-Year	10-Year
Cambridge Associates U.S. Private Equity Index (excluding venture capital)	11.3%	15.6%	15.8%	12.9%
Cambridge Associates U.S. Buyout Fund Index	13.8%	17.5%	16.9%	13.0%
Cambridge Associates U.S. Growth Equity Index	11.6%	16.4%	16.6%	13.0%
ILPA U.S. Private Equity Index (excluding venture capital)	11.2%	15.5%	15.8%	12.8%
PitchBook U.S. Private Equity Median Return (excluding venture capital)	9.8%	14.5%	13.9%	15.6%
Preqin Performance Analyst (including venture capital)	14.4%	15.7%	14.8%	16.9%
Preqin Performance Analyst (buyouts only)	14.5%	17.3%	16.1%	20.9%
Public Market Returns	**1-Year**	**3-Year**	**5-Year**	**10-Year**
Russell 3000 Index (including dividends)	12.6%	20.5%	15.6%	7.9%
S&P 500 Index (excluding dividends)	11.4%	17.9%	13.0%	5.4%
S&P 500 Index (including dividends)	13.7%	20.4%	15.5%	7.7%
Analysis	**1-Year**	**3-Year**	**5-Year**	**10-Year**
Median Private Equity Benchmark Return (excluding venture capital)[1]	11.2%	15.5%	15.8%	14.3%
Private Equity Benchmark Outperformance (excluding venture capital)[2]	-2.5%	-4.9%	0.3%	6.6%

Performance figures are based on most recent publicly available information.

Image 1.7. Private equity performance. Source: Preqin

As you can see, private equity and venture capital are quite different. If you haven't thought about this while deciding whether to pursue a venture capital career, then I highly encourage you to take a break from reading and spend a couple of days contemplating the difference between these two concepts. To make it more entertaining for you, watch the following movies to learn about private equity growth equity and buyouts:

- Other People's Money
- Pretty Woman
- Barbarians at the Gate

As for movies about venture capital, don't ruin your dream right away by watching the parody TV show "Silicon Valley". Instead, watch these:

- Startup dot com
- The Social Network
- Something Ventured

Not only do I think that some of you, dear readers, may change your minds and switch to pursuing a career in private equity, but I also believe that it is important to understand PE better, even if you decide to stick to venture investing anyway, because you'll likely have to work with private equity firms during later investment stages.

Where In The World You Can Build Your VC Career

In this first chapter, I am giving you a bird's eye view on the venture capital industry in different dimensions, and the geography of venture capital is one of them. Although most of the examples in this book come from venture capital practice in the United States, I do coach young investment professionals and aspiring VCs from various different countries. Aside from focusing on their local markets, I also try to keep their minds open and draw their attention to the specifics of other countries. Of course, many of them are interested in moving to the United States to work in VC, which is understandable, because the US is where the concept of venture capital was born, and is by far the largest venture capital market, with the highest concentration of venture dollars. Nevertheless, there are other centers for venture capital investment around the world where you can build your investing career with better odds, or at least other markets that you can focus on, and in so doing, build your expertise.

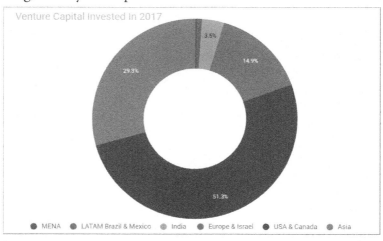

Image 1.8. Venture capital invested in 2017. Source: VC Academy

The first modern venture capital firm—American Research and Development (ARD)—was established in the United States in 1946. However, if we want to determine the beginning of the venture capital industry as we know it, it would be better to start from when the oldest venture firms that are still operating were established. Sequoia Capital and Kleiner Perkins Caufield & Byers (KPCB), for instance, both began in 1972. With this as a starting point, let's see when the venture capital industry was established in other countries.

Europe

Image 1.9. Activity in the European private equity market.
Source: EVCA/Thomson Venture Economics/PWC

Venture capital in Europe was initially driven by the boom in high-tech industries in the late 1990s and 2000. A significant number of early-stage European companies needed to be financed and nurtured, and venture capital was deemed the best solution for that. Although the governments of various European countries have made many attempts to provide startup companies with state-funded support, these programs could never replace or equally complement private venture money. The introduction of the single European currency, however, boosted the pan-European debt and equity markets significantly. It is fair to say that venture capitalization was born in Europe 20 years after the United States.

Maturation of the European venture capital arena was tough, however. Unlike the venture capital industry in the United States, which experienced tremendous growth in its early years, the European industry stagnated for more than a decade, and has only displayed meaningful changes recently.

"I've heard a series of explanations:
European economies are stagnant and rigid;
Europeans are status-conscious and risk-averse; all the action for
the mobile/cloud/digital-media economy is in Silicon Valley;
there are few good entrepreneurs in Europe."
Todd Hixon, Managing Partner at New Atlantic Ventures

Israel

When discussing the European venture capital industry, always specify whether Israel is included as part of it or not, because some sources do include Israel in Europe, but others don't. In 2017, $20.3 billion was invested in startups in Europe and Israel (of which $17.5 billion was in Europe alone). Israel has an older and more sophisticated venture capital industry than all of the other

European countries combined. When analysing the market, it makes more sense to review Israel together with Europe rather than with the Middle East, because the Middle Eastern venture capital market is relatively tiny, compared to the other countries.

Israel's venture capital industry was born in 1985, which is reportedly when the first Israeli venture capital fund, Athena Venture Partners, was founded by Major-General Dan Tolkowsky, former Chief of Staff of the Israeli Air Force. As in the United States, military needs and standards played a substantial role in the Israeli VC industry. The country has its own unique way of harvesting innovations and totally deserves to be a case study as an entrepreneurial and investment ecosystem.

The Israeli government initiative "Yozma" (Hebrew for "initiative"), implemented in 1993, offered attractive tax incentives to foreign venture capital investments in Israel, and promised to double any private investment with state funds. This is one of the many successful Israeli inventions in global venture capital practice.

Since then, Israel has been known worldwide for having the largest amount of venture capital invested per capita ($423 in 2015 vs $186 in the USA), as well as the highest value of exits per capita. Having raised only a third as much venture money as the UK in 2016 (€1.3 billion against €3.5 billion), Israel nevertheless surpassed the UK's amount of startup funding: local startups received over €4 billion in 2016 (almost double the amount received in 2015). This can be explained by the very high activity level of US venture capital firms in Israel.

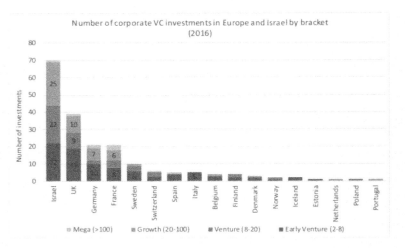

Image 1.10. Investment rounds in Israel with a US venture capital involved. Source: Geektime/Zirra

Asia

Asia, as a venture capital market, should be divided into four groups: (a) Japan and Korea; (b) Hong Kong (China), Singapore, and Taiwan (China); (c) Mainland China; and (d) developing Asia, which includes Indonesia, Malaysia, the Philippines, Thailand, and Vietnam. Given the dramatic differences in the stage of development and the size of these economies, it is not surprising that the size of the venture capital industries also differs, with most of the venture investments taking place in Mainland China (group C).

Aside from that, the region can be further subdivided into two categories: the "export-oriented" venture capital industries of Singapore and Hong Kong, which most closely resemble the industries of New York and London; and the "technology-oriented" industry of Taiwan, Mainland China, which most closely resembles the industry of Silicon Valley in the US.

Venture capital in China has grown steadily since the 1980s; in 2005, more than $1 billion was raised by Chinese venture capital firms—up from just $325 million in 2002. China represents one of the fastest growing markets for venture capital investing in the world, as Asia's large population displays a growing middle class and increasing appetite for consumer products and services. The combined Asian venture capital market invested $40 billion in 2017, which was second to the largest market in the world, that being the US and North American venture capital market with more than $73 billion invested in 2017, including $2.7 billion worth of investments made in Canada.

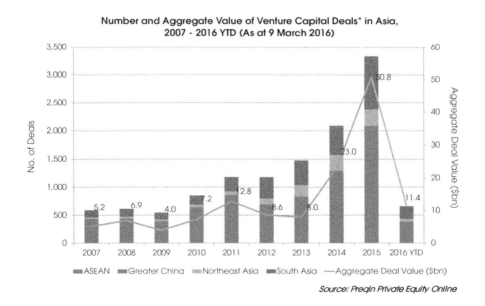

Source: Preqin Private Equity Online

Image 1.11. Number and aggregate value of venture capital deals in Asia, 2007-2016. Source: Preqin

Many reports include India as part of the Asian region, even though the Indian venture capital market is worthy of individual attention.

India

Indian financial authorities established the Risk Capital Foundation in 1975 to provide seed capital to small and risky projects. However, the concept of venture capital financing did not receive statutory recognition in the fiscal budget until 1986. Since then, Indian—primarily state-funded—venture firms started emerging, throughout the '90s, giving way to privately funded venture firms from the early 2000s. The volume of venture capital reached the $1 billion mark only 10 years after that, in 2012, and doubled again in 2015, reaching its record year in 2017 with $4.74B invested across the country.

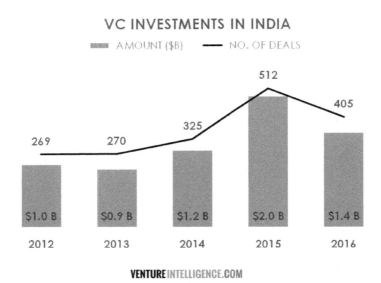

Image 1.12. Venture capital investments in India, 2012-2016.
Source: Ventureintelligence.com

The Indian venture capital industry remains poorly appreciated and even more poorly understood, despite the obvious potential of the Indian market with its booming middle class that is almost equal to the entire population of the United States. Hungry for tech innovations, Indian citizens aggressively consume everything the startup world has to offer. However, the local tech industry has been accused of harvesting ideas that are mere copycats of what has been proven in the USA and other countries. Well, if foreign companies can't make it to India, why shouldn't the country have its own problem-solvers?

Other serious doubts have been cast upon the rates of return realized by the venture funds investing in the Indian market. However, not only do Indian venture funds invest more and more money in local players, but international investors—such as Accel Partners and Sequoia Capital, as well as Chinese venture capitalists—are also rushing in with checks in hand. We can also see some Indian venture investors leaving their current employment with US venture firms and moving to India to work in their home market.

Other emerging centers of venture capital

Venture capital investments in Latin America (LATAM) and Middle East & North Africa (MENA), are still in their infancy, with an annual record that is still below $1 billion in each region. These regions didn't have such strong boosters as military budgets, as in the United States and Israel; therefore, venture capital in these countries merely follows entrepreneurs.

Local entrepreneurship, on the other hand, faces several early-stage challenges, such as:

- cost of failure
- limited management expertise
- lack of contacts or mentors
- lack of trust
- limited access to smart capital
- lack of role models

Understanding these limitations, venture capitalists keep their checkbooks ready, but their checks aren't fat enough yet. Maturing entrepreneurs and local populations hungry for innovation, definitely make LATAM and MENA very attractive, so everybody keeps watching these regions.

To get an instant overview of countries' attractiveness to venture capital, follow The Venture Capital and Private Equity Country Attractiveness Index, prepared annually by the Instituto de Estudios Superiores de la Empresa (IESE) Business School, Barcelona – University of Navarra, Spain.

Table 2: Regional VC and PE Attractiveness Landscape

Region	VC/PE Index	Economic Activity	Depth of Capital Market	Taxation	Investor Protection and Corporate Governance	Human and Social Environment	Entrepreneurial Culture and Deal Opportunities
1. North America	96,8	95,4	96,5	103,2	99,0	99,6	94,1
2. Australasia	89,2	84,8	82,8	107,8	104,6	98,5	83,9
3. West. Europe	78,7	78,5	70,6	112,7	85,3	83,0	78,9
4. Asia	69,1	88,8	65,1	95,9	69,6	61,0	64,9
5. Middle East	60,5	71,1	54,6	93,2	64,1	65,3	53,8
6. Eastern Europe	57,5	73,8	45,7	100,1	63,2	58,6	57,2
7. Latin America	51,5	72,0	45,9	86,6	53,0	46,5	46,2
8. Africa	43,0	62,9	31,2	82,8	54,8	46,1	39,0

Image 1.13. Regional venture capital and private equity attractiveness landscape. Source: Venture Capital and Private Equity Country Attractiveness Index

This index is designed to assess the six latent drivers of VC/PE attractiveness:

1. Economic Activity

2. Depth of Capital Market

3. Taxation

4. Investor Protection and Corporate Governance

5. Human and Social Environment

6. Entrepreneurial Culture and Deal Opportunities

A closer look at these drivers provides a very clear understanding of the factors that venture capitalists have to keep in mind when defining their geographical investment focus and making investment decisions.

Exhibit 1: The VC and PE Country Attractiveness Index – Construction Scheme

Venture Capital and Private Equity Country Attractiveness Index					
Economic Activity	Depth of Capital Market	Taxation	Investor Protection & Corporate Govern.	Human & Social Environment	Entrepren. Culture & Deal Opportunities
Total Economic Size (GDP)	Size of the Stock Market	Entrepren. Tax Inc. & Adm. Burdens	Quality of Corp. Governance	Education and Human Capital	Innovation
Expected Real GPD Growth	Market Cap of Listed Comp.	Entrepren. Incentive	Disclosure Index	Quality of Educational Sys.	Innovativeness Index
Unemployment	No. Listed Dom. Comp.	No. Tax Payments	Director Liability Index	Quality of Sci. Research Inst.	Capacity for Innovation
	SM Liquidity (Trading Volume)	Time spent on Tax Issues	Shareholder Suits Index	Labour Market Rigidities	Scientific & Tech. Journal Articles
	IPOs & Public Issuing Activity		Legal Rights Index	Difficulty of Hiring Index	Ease of Starting & Running a Business
	Market Volume		Efficacy of Corp. Boards	Rigidity of Hours Index	No. Procedures to start a Business
	Number of Issues		Security of Property Rights	Difficulty of Firing Index	Time needed to start a Business
	M&A Market Activity		Legal Enforce. of Contracts	Firing Costs	Costs of Bus. Start-Up
	Market Volume		Property Rights	Bribing and Corruption	Simplicity of Closing a Business
	Number of Deals		Intellectual Property Prot.	Bribing and Corruption Index	Time for Closing a Business
	Debt and Credit Market		Quality of Legal Enforcement	Control of Corruption	Costs for Closing a Business
	Ease of Access to Loans		Judicial Independence	Extra Payments/Bribes	Recovery Rate
	Credit Information Index		Impartial Courts		Corporate R&D
	Lending Rate		Integrity of the Legal System		R&D Spending
	Bank Non-Perf. Loans		Rule of Law		Utility Patents
	Financial Market Sophistication		Regulatory Quality		

Image 1.14. Venture capital and private equity country attractiveness index. Construction scheme. Source: Venture Capital and Private Equity Country Attractiveness Index

Do You Really Need To Be An Entrepreneur To Become A VC?

We have taken a peek at the place that venture capital occupies in the capital markets industry and the world, so let's now add you to the picture.

By far the most popular advice on how to become a venture investor is to become an entrepreneur first.

> *"When a young person asks me about getting in the venture capital business, I advise them not to. I think VC is an experienced person's game. Startups are not so much. Startups are a great place to be in your 20s and 30s.*
> *VC is a great place to be in your 40s and 50s."*
> *Fred Wilson, co-founding partner at Union Square Ventures*

Although this makes a lot of sense, the advice is quite lazy and uninspiring. Even a more creative version thereof, sounds doubtful:

> *"Venture capital is something to do at the end of your career, not the beginning.*
> *It should be your last job, not your first."*
> *Guy Kawasaki, marketing guru, author, investor*

Why? Entrepreneurial experience provides dozens of benefits for a VC career. However, being an entrepreneur before becoming a venture investor is not how many of the very prominent VCs did it, including Fred Wilson himself. My favorite example is Mike Moritz, a partner at Sequoia Capital, who jumped into venture capital straight after being a tech reporter. Jim Breyer, a partner at Accel, had been a management consultant before accepting an offer from the VC firm. Bill Gurley, a general partner at Benchmark, was a design engineer prior to starting a VC career. You can find a collection of VC career stories and advice on www.vc.academy where you will see even more unexpected scenarios of success from dozens of other VCs. Why is entrepreneurship still the first thing that comes to mind when discussing a venture capital career?

A study by Endeavour Insight Analytics showed that 40% of general partners at 30 top-tier VC firms had experience as founders of entrepreneurial companies, and the other 20% were senior executives at such companies. However, in a sample of randomly selected venture firms (not top-tier), only 27% of the partners had similar experience.

The study basically favors firms where the majority of partners who have entrepreneurial experience, over firms without such a profile. Although, the researchers admit that "it is obviously possible to find exceptional investors without entrepreneurial backgrounds", the study doesn't quite explain the connection between this profile and investing success or failure.

Entrepreneurial Experience Among Active General Partners

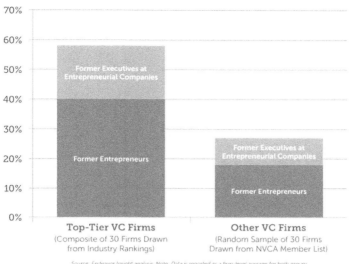

Image 1.15. Entrepreneurial experience among active general partners. Source: Endeavour Insight Analytics

Building your own company is "the easiest" way to acquire almost all the assets necessary—such as knowledge, skills, and even initial capital—for venture investing. You can build domain expertise, operational experience, and relationships, all of which would cover the entire investing process—from deal-sourcing through one's network, to growing and exiting a company. Those with operational entrepreneurial experience, who can also be called "operator VCs", may play a critical role in the success of a venture firm because they can reproduce their own entrepreneurial achievements working with portfolio companies, or help them avoid pitfalls and failures.

If this seems to you like the best way to go, just launch your own startup without any IPO goals and walk the same path as all startups do: regardless of the outcome, you'll get a lot of valuable insights and connections. It's a blunt way to go, but VCs like bold people after all.

To be fair, however, we should admit that many of these assets can be obtained without a personal entrepreneurial background (or being an executive of a startup, for that matter). For example, domain expertise may be a purely academic asset or it could be obtained while working in an operational role. A strong network can be built through many other ways, not to mention that legal and financial knowledge can easily be learned, as can almost any other hard skill. For all of this you only need a very strong self-discipline. What's left?

The only thing that there is absolutely no substitute for, is operational entrepreneurial experience, which provides inside knowledge and perspective on what it takes to make a company scale and succeed. This expertise is difficult to replicate in any other way.

Studies showed that "makers" (as in entrepreneurs) are better evaluators of new ideas than "managers". "Makers" tend to view their peers' ideas through the lens of: "How likely is this to succeed in the future?" instead of "How well does this act resemble what worked best in the past?". They never stop generating new ideas, which helps keep their minds open to novel ways to succeed. So the chances of people with entrepreneurial experience correctly recognizing a bright idea and accessing the likelihood of it being successful, are simply higher.

However, a good team of partners at a venture firm consists of people wearing different hats: operator, entrepreneur, generalist, specialist, strategist, and academic, etc. The formation of a team depends on the investment strategy of the fund. What stage is the venture fund going to invest in? Will the venture fund lead rounds? Will it be a passive or an active investor? Will its partners take board seats, and so on and so forth? Therefore, the significance of each of these roles may differ.

There are plenty of venture firms with partners who prefer to only sign the checks and don't want to be involved in the portfolio companies' operations. Hence, such firms may form a team from people with other competencies rather than entrepreneurial or operational experience. For example, partners of later-stage venture firms often come from investment banking and private equity: their experience in corporate matters is much more relevant at this point, because later-stage companies have passed the startup stage.

When looking for a VC job, you should try to understand what roles are valuable for the VC fund you'd like to join—which of them are filled already and where there may be a place for you. While operational experience is a strongly desirable and critical asset, it is not always a must-have. You can be brilliant and become an irreplaceable team member without it too. If you don't have an entrepreneurial background, design your own way of bringing value—for example, become a domain expert or develop your strategic acumen. In addition to listing your soft and hard skills, which we'll discuss further, your resume should provide a clear idea on which of the possible hats you can wear as a VC team member.

Let's also look at entrepreneurial experience from another angle. Being an entrepreneur alone doesn't guarantee that you'll land a VC job. This is something that you won't read about in interviews with VCs and other articles with career advice often. There's a lot of other work to do at a venture firm, besides picking winners, at which you can become indispensable.

Graduating from a top university has nothing to do with becoming a successful VC either: an entrepreneur would much rather meet with an associate who has some operational experience to share or domain knowledge, than with an MBA graduate who has neither. This hard truth has been mentioned by different investment professionals and entrepreneurs here and there, but hasn't affected the job descriptions much: many VC firms still have that education filter in place.

Check out the Venture Capital Aptitude Test (VCAT) created by Guy Kawasaki. Although it's more for fun than as a true assessment, it can give you some examples of the skills an entrepreneur can use in venture capital.

ASSIGNMENT 1

At the beginning of the coaching program, we reflect on the basics of the venture capital industry. We determine a level of understanding of the investing practices and capital markets of each coachee and discuss what they've learned from the introductory lessons, which are also the first chapter of this book. Here are some of the questions I ask, and exercises we do:

1. Find systems in your daily life.
2. What can you start investing in, in the short term?
3. Which investment philosophy is closer to you: growth capital and private equity buyouts or venture capital investing?
4. What geographical markets are you interested in learning about and working in?
5. If you don't have entrepreneurial experience, what other superpowers do you have?

To access the section with the additional materials on my website, please, use the password **VCmind$et**.

CHAPTER 2

CREATING YOUR INVESTOR PROFILE

Find Yourself As A Venture Investor

I hope you've had a great movie night or two by now. Without further ado, let's start working on your future in venture capital!

They say that some VC firms are looking for candidates with literally zero experience, so that they can train them from scratch. I haven't seen any job openings like this yet. If this was true, then such a person would start from the youngest position possible— let's say an analyst—and the list of requirements for such a hire is officially pretty lengthy. In the absolute majority of these cases, VCs are looking for someone with basic knowledge (often exaggerated in the resume) and a sense of purpose in mind. This chapter is dedicated to finding yourself in a venture capital career. I want you to speak with confidence when you are talking to a partner of a VC firm. Regardless of the depth of your knowledge, if you show that you know what you are looking for in venture investing, and who you would like to become, it will set you up for a profound conversation. Venture investors typically love mentoring, so who knows—maybe by showing your desirable future self, you will make the interviewing partner want to have an apprentice like you.

Saying that you want to become a venture investor is like saying "I want to become a doctor". We all know that there are different kinds of doctors out there and although they study the same textbooks early in their career, an ophthalmologist would be pretty useless at a dentist's office.

Venture capitalists are as different as doctors in several aspects. Not only do they invest in different industries—an IT investor wouldn't invest in pharmacology, for example—but they also have different stage and geography preferences, as well as distinct missions and individual approaches.

Throughout this chapter, we'll be discussing the elements that define a venture investor—or in venture speak, the investor profile.

The term "investor profile" is most often applied to self-directed investors in public stock, and defines one's preferences in investment decisions. When used in venture capital, it would include your preferred industry and geography investment focus, the stage of the companies' lifecycles that you'd prefer to invest at, the type of support you could provide your portfolio companies with, and a high-level description of the products/services and type of entrepreneurs you'd like to back. Some of these preferences may reflect your motives and drives, and you can also include your mission statement.

What does "investor profile" have to do with you if you are at the very beginning of your career path and haven't invested anything as yet? You are reading this book so that you can become a more desirable candidate for a VC firm. Firstly, the chances of a greenhorn being hired, are much lower than those of a rookie who, at the very least, knows the direction that he or she is heading in at that moment, even though it might eventually change. Secondly, an investor profile will make your job search more meaningful: instead of blindly sending your CV to hundreds of VC firms with no results—also known as "spraying and praying" (an investment strategy of investing small amounts in many startups in the hope that a few of them will become winners)—you'll be able to make more big bets (another investment strategy of picking the most promising companies for your specific portfolio of investments).

Designing an investor profile is the most intensive part of my coaching program. It requires a lot of learning and brainstorming, but it is also the part where my coachees have the most fun! As promised, every reader of this book gets access to the worksheets we use during my program. You are welcome to download them from my website and try to work on creating your investment profile yourself.

An investor profile should make your job interviews go smoother, and allow you to answer such tricky questions as "Why do you want to become a venture investor?" or "What would you invest in and why?" We'll be talking more about the components of your investor profile further in this chapter, but here is a spoiler. There is no right or wrong investor profile. However you see yourself, your profile should be narrow enough to make you a desirable candidate, but broad enough to keep other doors open.

Telling your story right is important in many industries, and venture capital is no exception. That's why hundreds of qualified investment professionals cannot find jobs quickly enough or are not getting hired at all—they just don't put the right words together. Your public profile, your CV, and you yourself at an interview, should clearly show that you know what you are talking about and what it is you want.

An investor profile has little to do with your resume. Yes, you can, of course, mention some of your core competencies, especially if your portfolio companies can benefit from them, but your resume is like a manual compared to an advertising pamphlet, which is what your investor profile should become. Don't take it too literally though.

You can choose any presentation manner for your investor profile, however, I advise you not to overdo it. I've seen candidates paying to have professional slides designed, or even infographics. Although it looks impressive, what you say is far more important than which font you use.

When looking for a job, some applicants create presentation decks to pitch their candidacy, instead of a resume, which becomes a secondary document and is either attached to the deck or sent separately if requested. Such presentation decks are sometimes called "investment theses" to show that the candidate speaks the same language as a potential employer—a general partner who also presents an investment thesis to the limited partners.

From the very first moment you start building your career in venture capital, you are looking for your place in the system. Information about you should be available and relevant to potential employers and recruiters, other VCs and aspiring investors, entrepreneurs whom you may advise or invest in at some point, event organizers, journalists, and other prospective partners. Although they have different interests, you need to show the value you can create for each of them in very few words. Therefore, your positioning and message should be very neat.

Whatever you declare about your investment preferences at an interview with a potential employer, needs to be consistent with your public profile. We all ask Google about our new acquaintances, let alone potential employees or partners, so social media should only confirm that you're confident in your position to make it public.

Creating a professional self throughout different mediums is not an easy task, and because you want to target different audiences, there is a lot to keep in mind.

In our hyperconnected world, we all need to be consistent with what we preach. Your investor profile is not an exception. When designing your investor profile, don't forget that parts or all of it should be public. It's hard to avoid displaying yourself and translating your message on the web, especially early in your career, because you need to create your industry presence, and social media is the fastest way to do it.

An investor profile is not set in stone and may change over time, especially if you are an aspiring investor. That is why I advise my coachees on specific wording that will keep the door open to other opportunities. For instance, if you know a thing or two about blockchain, it should be clear to your potential employer, but you probably want to show that this is not the only sector that you are interested in. When talking about the preferred industry or sector investment focus, it makes sense to tell your story so that you can explain why you have been historically passionate about those you are already familiar with, and why you want to deepen your knowledge about others.

Finally, it is also important to not confuse the community with your investor status if you are not actually investing, or end up in a different industry after all. There were times when every wannabe VC referred to themselves as investors, without having a dime to actually invest. Others called themselves advisors and were collecting a stock of naïve entrepreneurs in exchange for useless recommendations. Some actors were real frauds, and they used this as a cover-up to steal ideas and proprietary information from startups.

The industry, as a system, has cleaned itself up a great deal, and has gotten rid of most of these types of parasites, however, we can still sometimes bump into them here and there. You don't want to create even the slightest suspicion regarding yourself. The proper wording for an investor profile is critical for protecting your public image in the long term.

I will deliberately not expand on such areas as copyrighting, networking, or social media marketing in this version of the book, because it would distract you from its main purpose. While I help with this during individual coaching sessions, let's just agree for now that you will definitely need some writing and presentation skills to create your investor profile. If in doubt, you are welcome to send me your draft, as I have promised to reply to the first email from each of my readers. With all of this in mind, let's start building your investor profile step by step.

Understanding What's Right For You

I have already challenged your decision to work in venture capital once, by suggesting that you consider private equity instead. In this book, I will keep trying to convince you that venture capital is not for you. Why am I doing this? Not only do I aim to bring new talent into venture capital, but I also want them to survive in the industry and leave their footprints. Venture capital is a very fashionable occupation today—sexy, as they say. However, it requires a lot of unsexy qualities, such as patience, discipline, and persistence. There are no quick rewards in venture capital, and the first excitement that one experiences when being called an "investor", goes away pretty quickly. If you lose your enthusiasm about pursuing a career in venture capital by the third chapter, I'll have saved you wasted time from looking in the wrong direction, or maybe even wasting years on something that you aren't really passionate about. If nothing that this book tells you scares you away, then I'll be happy to support you further.

People think that belonging to the tribe of venture capitalists not only proves to the world that you are wealthy, but also gives you power, because you affect the lives of others seeking funding for their businesses. More importantly, you can share the glory if they succeed, even if you barely did anything yourself. We see so many leaders—partners and other executives—of venture funds living that lifestyle!

Is this what primarily attracts you to venture capital?

Be honest with yourself. If this is your main motivation, you should probably consider a different direction.

Even if you feel good about yourself and your career choice, as described above, it doesn't mean that other people will feel the same way about you—especially, your fellow venture investors. For starters, a venture fund has a very specific salary structure, and your income will reflect your skills as an investor, which they are very aware of. Moreover, your investment in a startup may be the first or the largest, but it doesn't automatically mean that it will become a turning point on the startup's road to success. Finally, your impact in the startup's life can only be proven over time, so even if you played a significant role in its success, there's no quick recognition of that. Truth be told, unless you're an executive of a venture fund or an individual investor yourself, the chances that you'll receive public appreciation are low.

Sounds demoralizing, right? Exactly! Venture capital is a long shot. Because the results of your investment decisions are delayed, you need motivation that won't fade over time.

Of course, there may be short-term interest in a venture capital job, like adding a line that will look good on your CV and getting "street cred". You'll learn or practice a couple of useful skills along the way too, but altogether, it won't make you part of the tribe.

To be fair, everything I have listed above is normal human nature. After all, most people are inclined to seek personal recognition consciously or subconsciously. Nothing's wrong with that. What matters are the main motives.

Knowing your "whys" is important for succeeding in life—whether personal or professional. In this chapter we'll discuss the many layers of motivation, the necessary qualifications, and the responsibilities required for working in venture capital.

Let's start with the primary drives, which have been cited most frequently among all of the possible motives of venture investors:
- money
- passion
- curiosity.

Making Money

Whether you're an angel investor, a venture capitalist, or a corporate venture investor (we'll address the differences later), multiplying invested capital is the ultimate goal. Even if you want to bring innovations to the world and are concerned about social good, the return on investment matters. You probably think that philanthropy, as a form of investing, doesn't set certain material goals. It does. It's only charities that have no expectations of financial returns.

Emotions and intentions aside, a venture capitalist is eventually judged by the returns he or she makes on an invested dollar. If this approach isn't the one you wake up with, but you still want to be an investor, consider other forms of investing.

Passion for Building Businesses

If you don't have experience or simply don't like building businesses (nothing shameful in this), you can achieve returns comparable to that of venture capital, or even higher returns, by investing in a stock exchange or somewhere between these two investing fields—in private equity. Be open—there are other ways and means to become a successful investor.

In venture capital, even if you're the "silent" type of investor who signs the checks, but doesn't participate in the operations of portfolio companies, passion for watching a business grow will set you on the right track. Otherwise, you can grow impatient expecting results faster than a business can produce, and you can become unsatisfied with your job.

However, because there are a lot of venture dollars in the market, it's entrepreneurs who make choices and they often prefer to work with investors who are instrumental in achieving success faster. This is where prior business or tech experience, network, product and management advice, or your other superpowers, may make you stand out among other investors.

Intellectual Curiosity

Becoming a successful venture capitalist won't happen simply because you've read all the right books or received an Ivy League MBA. Intellectual curiosity, however, is considered the most important quality that can make or break an investor's career, and it has nothing to do with your previous working experience either.

Venture capital is a business of uncertainty. There's no crystal ball to predict whether a technology, innovation, product, or service will fly, and to what heights (in other words, what would be the return on this investment). What makes some venture capitalists better than others is their skill at asking questions. Gifted investors try to look at a startup from different angles—even angles that the founders themselves haven't considered.

One of my favorite questions starts with, "What if...?". What if we position this differently? What if we use an unconventional channel to attract users? What if we pick a different market to compete in? There's no list of such questions, nor are there right or wrong answers. There's no education that can build this skill strongly enough. Even prior business or tech experience can't ensure that a person becomes intellectually curious. One can, however, try to develop it, and I want to guide you in this endeavour with this book.

I've already mentioned Michael Moritz, a general partner of one of the best venture capital firms worldwide, Sequoia Capital. Representing Sequoia, he invested in companies such as Google, Yahoo, PayPal, Kayak, and Zappos.com, with dozens of other winners. Before his venture capital career, he worked as a correspondent for The Times and wrote several books.

Journalism is one of the professions where system thinking is trained on a daily basis. Michael is a prime example of an unconventional venture capital career path, which only confirms that **it's the mindset that matters—not your bio.**

This should encourage you to play by your own rules in venture capital!

Now that you understand the main priorities of a venture investor, note that the goal of this chapter is to have you question whether venture capital is a good match for you on a personal level. Your passion for venture investing will either grow over the pages, or it will evaporate. Each of these outcomes will result in my mission being accomplished.

Personal Returns That Matter To You

Aside from those must-have motives that we discussed on a previous page, that you would need if you want to become a dedicated venture investor, there may be many other motivations and drives. Before we start building your investor profile and making you a desirable candidate for venture capital funds, it is critical that you learn to understand yourself better.

"The investors we hire and the founders we back are the same in one important regard: they have a desperate need to win."

Pat Grady, Partner at Sequoia

You now know the differences between two close investment concepts—private equity and venture capital. You've checked to see whether you possess the primary drives, such as making money, building businesses, and being profoundly curious. Now, I want you to add more layers to your motives. I've put together a whole list of potential motivations. It is by no means exhaustive, but nevertheless is a solid foundation for your career map.

Many attempts have been made to explore the motivations of people who invest in risky enterprises. If venture capital only chases profit, aren't there many other less risky ways to get it? What do individuals and organizations hope to achieve from their investments of money, time, and other resources, with no guarantee of return? What drives them? What are their expectations? Of course, the answers to these questions are as varied as the people themselves, so when exploring your own investor profile, don't limit yourself to the list of motives suggested in this chapter—try to look beyond it, to find at least one motivation that we don't mention here.

In their book, "Measuring and Improving Social Impacts", Marc J. Epstein and Kristi Yuthas try to explain what drives people to invest in a social cause, especially when financial returns may not be in the picture at all. The authors offer four groups of drives that move impact investors:

Identity returns	Process returns
• Reciprocity • Satisfaction • Reputation	• Knowledge • Experience • Relationships
Financial returns	**Social impact**
• Profits • Increase in value	• Societal • Environmental

Image 2.1. Main drives for impact investors. Source: "Measuring and Improving Social Impacts", Marc J. Epstein, Kristi Yuthas

Although this matrix is related to impact investors, the social factor takes place in almost all of today's venture investments—at least, for the sake of positioning and marketing. Therefore, we can still use this matrix, while keeping in mind that impact as a motive will likely carry a smaller weight than motives from other groups. We won't focus on the financial motivation in this context either, because we've already figured out that it belongs to the very first layer of motives for venture investing. Instead, you should now explore your personal and emotional reasons for investing, that aren't effectively captured in terms of financial or social returns.

As mentioned earlier, most of the possible rewards from venture investing—like satisfaction and reputation—only happen over time, and can be as significant for a person as the obvious monetary return on invested capital. That's why it's easy to put all these motives and drives into one dimension and think about all of them as returns that are equal in importance to financial motivation.

Identity Returns

Identity returns are a direct and often personal reflection on the identity of the individual or organization making the investment, from the inside, as well as from the outside. Different motives may fall into this category—from altruistic to egocentric. The matrix suggests focusing on three main motives:

- *Reciprocity.* The sense of obligation to repay the community for one's good fortune. Many general and limited partners of venture funds, as well as angel investors, who were successful entrepreneurs themselves, often name their "desire to return back to the community" by investing in entrepreneurs like themselves.
- *Satisfaction.* The emotional benefits associated with the act of making the investment. Feelings of power, wealth, and significance, as discussed in the previous lecture, fall into this category.
- *Reputation.* Community recognition and branding resulting from alignment with certain investments.

Needless to say, people making financial decisions have always been treated as superiors, and the investment field is probably the easiest way to build such a reputation (never try to fake it though—it is easily identified and won't be forgiven by the community).

Process Returns

Process returns are those benefits that flow from the process of engagement in a project. This book offers three broad categories of process returns:

- *Knowledge.* The information and learning acquired by investing in or working with an organization. Intellectually curious people appreciate the learning opportunities offered by venture investing.

- *Experience.* The skills and understanding gained as a result of investments. There are many venture investors who have never been entrepreneurs themselves. They have different areas of expertise, and this works perfectly for their portfolio companies. Such investors can get hands-on experience of building a business from scratch and scale this experience to new investments, or even their own companies when they trade a VC career for becoming an entrepreneur (oh yes, I'll tell you such stories further in the book).

- *Relationships.* Personal or business relationships formed or strengthened by the collaboration with a target investment. New relationships and networking opportunities are an integral part of the investing process, since venture capital is never a lone wolf game (although, it may feel lonely—we'll talk about this later).

At this point, you should have a dozen or more words in mind that could describe your motivation. If some of them aren't mentioned above, that's great! Like I said, it's impossible to cover all possible motives and drives, so while the matrix gives us a broader frame, there's another list of motivations I'd like to share with you.

Bonnie Foley-Wong suggested the following drives of venture investors, which may or may not repeat or echo those I've mentioned above:

- *Status*: To be the person who discovers the next big thing, to be the talent-spotter.
- *Power*: To influence and have power over business decisions.
- *Leadership*: To empower and help others and provide vision and direction.
- *Connection*: To connect with other investors and be part of an investor community.
- *Security*: To create financial security through the accumulation of assets and reserves, to manage an uncertain future.
- *Future Consumption*: To enable future consumption through the accumulation of resources that grow, multiply, and can be used in the future to purchase goods and services.

- *Obsolescence*: To prepare for products and services that are no longer useful, nor serve a purpose.
- *Innovation*: To proactively develop products and services that are useful and serve us better in the future.
- *Legacy*: To provide for future generations.
- *Making Decisions*: To gather new information or create new tools to help us make decisions.
- *Exchange*: To provide a means of exchange in the form of money, shares, or other financial instruments.

I should stop here and allow you to continue the list yourself. Download a template of the matrix from my website, so that you can write down your own motives and drives, and rate them according to the significance they have for you personally. Having this list will help you to better understand what your career and investment decisions should be based on. This, in turn, will help you seek very specific characteristics in startups, at the stage of the first pitch, and remain satisfied with the investment, even if it doesn't become a success story—because it has been consistent with your values.

I have already mentioned that an investor profile defines an individual's preferences in investment decisions. Although, people usually use this term when referring to such investment preferences as industry, stage, or geography, I believe that on a personal level, motives should be included in your investor profile too, at least for yourself. In the long term, knowing them will simply make you a more successful investor.

There's no better or worse profile—each person's investment profile is unique. You will discover that some motives and drives are more important than others for a particular investment decision. Also, don't let the overlap of different motives, and the interactions between them, confuse you—that happens, and it's perfectly normal.

Investors Belong To Different Tribes

When pursuing a career in venture capital, it may be helpful to understand the differences between the various types of venture investors, namely: angel investors, venture capitalists, corporate venture investors, and a relatively new type of investor—scouts. There is now also the most recently created tribe of crypto investors among venture capitalists, but that requires a separate book.

Let's start with **corporate venture investing**, as this may become the quickest way for some of you to get into venture capital. If you currently work for a corporation, pay attention to any of its activities that may be referred to as "corporate business development". Although the word "venture" is not mentioned at all here, the objectives of this corporate force may not only be directed towards mergers and acquisitions, but also at investments in equity, that are paid for with corporate money. The number of companies that are strengthening their corporate business development front is probably at a record high at the moment. If your company does not have corporate business development activities in place, initiate them yourself by suggesting it to your bosses. Approach your future venture capital career unconventionally and take the initiative—even if you become the only person involved.

You may be wondering what the differences between corporate venture capital (CVC) and traditional venture capital are.

One obvious difference is the source of the capital. Traditional venture funds raise money from several limited partners, which may or may not include corporations. Corporate venture capital funds use their parent company's money as a major source of funding, and although other participating limited partners may join, it doesn't happen often.

The reason for this is that, unlike traditional VCs that invest for financial returns, CVCs tend to have strategic objectives that are aligned with the core business of their parent companies. When the concept of CVC was first implemented, many corporate venture funds invested with a goal of future acquisitions, which often resulted in the acquired companies being shut down or stopped from further development. When entrepreneurs realized that "there is no life after a merger", many of them started deciding against CVCs when investments were offered. Once this trend became strong enough, CVCs went vocal about changes that had been made to their strategies, in order to win the entrepreneurs over. Generally speaking, CVCs currently invest less with the intention of M&A, and more with the goal of either complementing the core product or business, or dealing with competitors with the help of portfolio companies in one way or another. Therefore, return on invested capital is not the first concern for corporate venture investors.

One more difference to keep in mind, is the spotty track record that CVCs have in terms of follow-up investments, which often happens due to strategy and leadership changes.

Finally, CVCs typically don't require tight control over portfolio companies, partly due to fiduciary responsibilities and accounting implications. They are, however, often willing to give their portfolio companies access to many of its resources.

Another type of venture investors that are rarely talked about, are the **"scouts"**. This is the "hottest club" in Silicon Valley these days, which was started by Sequoia Capital several years back, and has resulted in several other funds experimenting with their versions of such a program today. Some of the venture firms that have launched such programs are: Accel Partners, CRV, Founders Fund, Index Ventures, Lightspeed Venture Partners, Social Capital, and Spark Capital, according to people who are familiar with the concept. Although many funds have been trying to keep their programs a closely guarded secret in order to get an advantage with promising startups, some firms have decided to maintain their transparency in this regard. For example, Flybridge Capital and First Round Capital have announced public versions of such programs.

Because this is quite an innovative approach to early-stage venture investing often employed by larger venture firms with as much as a billion dollars under management and more, the format of scout programs varies. The initial model deems scouts as "individuals using money fully or partially fronted by a VC fund, in order to make investments in early-stage companies with hopes of giving the sponsoring fund an advantage in leading a larger round for the startup later on". It seems like a great idea to be able to become a venture investor without investing your own money and pitching hundreds of institutional investors like many general partners of traditional venture funds do, right?

Aside from this convenience, scouts also have a very strong financial motivation, as they keep the upside from the deals, if any. According to Jason McCabe Calacanis, the returns split between the parties of the Sequoia scout program look like this:

- 45% to the scout
- 50% to Sequoia
- 5% to a pool for all the other scouts

Sequoia's follow-on investments in such well-known companies as Stripe and Thumbtack, both currently valued in billions, were originated by scouts. You can therefore see how significant an upside could be for a scout.

Becoming a scout seems like a very attractive opportunity, however it's obvious that venture firms would never entrust their money to an unknown individual, so the chances of becoming one as an outsider, are tiny. Some time ago, venture funds created the "entrepreneur-in-residence" (EIR) position, which was for the hiring of experienced entrepreneurs who could help portfolio companies with growth and other operational problems that they are good at solving. Some of these EIRs, in fact, became the first scouts. Another way to become a scout with a large VC firm, is to be an angel investor yourself—your interests may then be perfectly aligned with the VC firm.

At this point, it makes sense to say a couple of words about getting into venture capital as an **angel investor**.

Having your own track record as an angel investor is one of the most reliable paths towards being hired by a venture firm, or raising your own fund. Of course, this does require you to have enough savings in order to allocate a portion of them to risky investing, and not being afraid of losing it entirely, but it doesn't mean you have to invest millions. If you become a part of a syndicate, your individual investment in a startup could be as low as $5,000, which is doable if you are switching from working for a big corporation or Wall Street. If none of the other strategies for getting into venture capital works, refuel your patience, start saving specifically for angel investing, and continue learning about venture capital.

To become an attractive employee for a venture capital firm, you won't need to wait until your angel portfolio companies become "unicorns". Your portfolio and investor profile will speak for themselves among venture capitalists who may like them and invite you to join their firm. As you can see, motivation for angel investing can also be different: are you building your portfolio just as a means to work for or start your own venture fund, or is this is the way of investing you prefer?

How is angel investing different from investing through a **traditional venture fund**? The shortest answer was given by an angel investor, Joanne Wilson: "I never say never, but I am absolutely 100% positive that I will never take other people's capital to invest for several reasons. First and foremost is I don't want to be held accountable to my LP's or anyone. It is that simple." Ironically, her husband is Fred Wilson, a co-founding partner at Union Square Ventures. So she knows what she's talking about.

Although a venture fund doesn't legally guarantee any returns, and could very well burn all the money, leaving its limited partners with nothing, the future of its general partners in this scenario may be doomed. Managing a venture fund is a long-term game. After the first fund, general partners typically raise another venture fund, and then the next, and all over again. If you failed miserably with your first venture fund, the odds of raising another fund and being invited as a partner into any other fund are... well, modest. The third fund after another failure? From very low to zero. Of course, venture capital has the image of being the most tolerant industry towards failures, however, in practice, you'll have to prove hard that your failure was the exception and not the rule, and that you deserve another try. Because 'failure' is the middle name of venture capital, you'd better think about this scenario upfront.

I have been an angel investor, a general partner, and the managing director of a corporate venture fund myself, and can attest to their core differences. I have learned which tribe I belong to and which model matches my character better. That is why I have written this book—to show you the system of the venture capital industry and to help you find your place in it.

Define Your Mission

Up until this point, we have only touched on the basics of what it means to become a venture investor. Although it may seem like parental lecturing, don't skip this: everything that we've discussed can help you design your mission statement as an investor. After all, venture investors have considerable power when it comes to money, connections, and decision-making that can change humanity—so what will keep us accountable in terms of using these powers?

If you, like me, find the word "mission" too pompous, please feel free to replace it with a more attractive name, such as: purpose, vision, framework, aim, ambition, or calling (there is a well-developed technique for creating a mission statement, so I'll be using the original terminology to avoid any confusion). Regardless of what people call it, you may not know what you are doing, but you certainly need to know why you are doing it.

This "why" is the most important product I work on with aspiring venture investors during my coaching program. The exercise involves some extensive brainstorming and self-discovery that you would normally need to do with a coach, but I will attempt to give you the direction you will need in order to try and do it yourself.

Among the many reasons for creating a mission statement, which you can find on the internet, the most important reasons for our discussion are the following:

1. A mission statement brings clarity to all the actions and decisions you make, and keeps you going when you feel like hope is deserting you.
2. A mission statement is what you pitch when you are looking for a job.

Uncertainty is an integral component of venture investing, therefore, any tool that helps you make decisions—including the ultimate one regarding your career in venture capital—should not be underestimated. You'll have plenty of challenging moments in venture investing. Even if none of your portfolio companies survive, if your investment decisions were directed by a mission you truly believe in, then you will not regret the time and money spent, and will instead find the upside.

What is a professional mission statement? Out of all the available definitions, the one given by Project Manager Coach, Susanne Madsen, is the best:

"A mission statement is a paragraph that encapsulates everything you would like to be, do, and have in your career. It defines what success and excellence look like to you. It expresses your vision for where you want to be in the future, and it reflects your values, goals, and purpose, and how you want to operate."

This can be applied to a lifelong personal or professional path in general (not without adjustments once in a decade). For example, Oprah Winfrey's mission statement is: "To be a teacher. And to be known for inspiring my students to be more than they thought they could be"; and Richard Branson's: "To have fun in [my] journey through life and learn from [my] mistakes".

If you haven't created such a mission statement for yourself yet, I encourage you to think about it during your quiet times or after hours. This book and my coaching program, however, focus on your mission statement as a venture investor, so let's look at some relevant examples:

"I'm interested in the increasing rate of change caused by technology, in all market segments."
Doug Leone, Partner at Sequoia

"My mission is getting money into the hands of people that should already have it, but have been ignored or underestimated."
Arlan Hamilton, founder of Backstage Capital

"I want to work on things that will last for decades and that will transform how people work, live, and play."
Carl Eschenbach, Partner at Sequoia

"Create clarity in the world of startups."
Johan van Mil, Founder and Managing Partner at Peak Capital

Digging deeper into this subject, there are several slightly different types of statements you need to recognize. There are mission and vision statements that can be personal or professional. Since we are definitely working on the professional one, let's only define the difference between mission and vision statements.

A **vision statement** is focused more on the future. It defines the optimal desired future state—the mental picture—of what you want to achieve over time, e.g. in five, ten, or more years. It answers the question "Where do I want to be?".

Neutral example: "My vision is a world where everyone is contributing their full potential; where each person uses their intrinsic genius and leadership to deliver outstanding value-added projects."
Carl Eschenbach's statement would fall into the vision statement category.

A **mission statement** talks about the present leading to the future, and answers the question: "How will I get to where I want to be?" among others, e.g. "What do I do?", "How do I do it?", "Who do I do it for?", "What makes me different?", and "What is the benefit?".

Neutral example: "My mission is to help project managers transform into impactful project leaders."
Arlan Hamilton's statement sounds more like a mission statement.

Many people don't realize that they already have a mission statement. It may be a daily mantra or a favorite quote, which we call "words to live by", but because we want to define your professional mission, let's not sink into plagiarism.
A simplified template that serves the purpose of developing your own mission statement as a future venture capitalist, links together only three elements:

the value you create + who you're creating it for + the expected outcome

Neutral example: "I use my passion and expertise in technology to inspire researchers to create drugs to cure rare diseases".

Because we have already reflected on your values and motivations earlier in the chapter, you should be able to craft your mission statement without too much trouble.

As I said previously, a mission statement is more concerned about the present than the future (that's why, for the purpose of a job search, I prefer to work on a mission statement rather than a vision statement). As such, it should be revisited and adjusted as your life circumstances change, because they will. A mission statement is not the Ten Commandments for the rest of your life, and should only project the foreseeable future (approximately three to five years).

To illustrate this... I updated my own mission statement a couple of years ago when I realized that I had become truly passionate about professional education in venture investing. Today I'm directed by the following purpose: "Bring more emerging managers into the venture capital industry by making the relevant knowledge and collective experience more accessible and comprehensible." I haven't done everything that I am capable of and what I have in mind, yet, however, so stay tuned. This book is one of a dozen projects on my list to finish before I'll get to adjust my purpose again. To get the most out of it, please close it now and take a couple of days to reflect on everything you've read so far.

Specialists Or Generalists?

Now that we have discovered the personal side of you as an investor, let's speak about the professional side of your investor profile.

Regardless of what position you are applying for in a VC firm, sooner or later you will have to think about the industry or sector you would like to learn more about, and invest in. Should you focus on just one thing or many? Isn't just one focus too narrow? How many focuses are enough? And how many is too many? The best way to address this issue is to approach it as experienced venture capitalists do.

When it comes to industry investment focus, venture investors on both levels—firm and personal—belong to two different tribes: specialists and generalists.

The Merriam-Webster dictionary defines a generalist as "a person who knows something about a wide range of things". A specialist is defined as "a person who has special knowledge and skill relating to a particular job or area of study".

In venture capital, sector specialists invest the majority of their capital in a couple of related sectors or within a particular industry. For example, Autotech Ventures describes themselves as: "a specialist firm focused on investing in revolutionary transportation technologies and business models targeting the $3 trillion ground transportation market." Or Anterra Capital, who mention it on the first page of their website: "We are a specialist venture capital investor dedicated to financing the growth of companies operating in the food & agricultural sectors".

Generalist venture capital firms are the "jacks of all trade"—they are open to invest in any industry as long as they find the pitching startup promising, thereby diversifying their investments across various industries.

Historically, biopharma- and life-science-focused venture capital firms were the only specialists. Most of the first US venture firms invested in pretty much anything new and promising, even if they had been focused, let's say, on semiconductors, at inception. However, today, clear industry focus (even if that includes several unrelated industries) is a must-have for any investment theses of a venture fund, and more and more venture firms prefer to position themselves as specialists. Here is why: extensive research has proven that specialist venture capital firms outperform generalist VCs.

"This outperformance comes from the intimate knowledge of an industry – in an increasingly competitive private equity environment, a manager's ability to demonstrate deep expertise in a focused field is a key differentiator."
Andrea Auerbach, Managing Director and Global Head of Private Investment Research at Cambridge Associates

We know, however, that top VC firms, such as Kleiner, Perkins, Caufield, and Byers (KPCB) and Sequoia Capital are definitely generalists. How does this make sense then? Let's dig deeper.

KPCB, one of the leading venture capital firms, is a generalist firm comprised largely of generalists such as John Doerr, who has made investments in the internet (Amazon, Google), computer software (Intuit), and computer hardware (Sun Microsystems). The same goes for Sequoia Capital. Some generalist VC firms are comprised of venture capitalists who are themselves generalists, while others are comprised of a diversified group of industry specialists.

Research has shown that specialization at the individual level is more important than specialization at the firm level, and venture capital firms with specialist partners are more successful, whether those firms position themselves as generalists or specialists.

Along with that, the best overall and industry-adjusted performance is associated with more generalist venture capital firms, however only if they are mature enough. Venture capital firms with more experience tend to outperform those with less experience, and both firm- and personal-level industry experience matters for investment success. In other words, if a venture firm is young, it had better be a specialist if it wants to be successful. But if a firm is mature, it may be even more successful as a generalist firm.

Now let's pay attention to individual specialization. The poorest performance is associated with unspecialized firms with generalist investors. Therefore, generalist venture firms should have more specialists among the partners than generalists. If you read about every team member of Sequoia Capital on its website, you'll see exactly that composition. Specialized venture capital firms, however, should keep a healthy balance of specialists and generalists, because excessive specialization may mean a lack of relevant expertise or deal access in other promising sectors.

So, unless you are an experienced investment professional, you want to position yourself as a specialist. As the research pointed out, excessive specialization is not good, so you need to find the right balance. An obvious and correct first choice, is to specialize in something you are truly passionate about. In this case, your passion will make you an expert, regardless of whether your education is relevant to this specialty. Then, experiment with subjects you have learned at school or university, but are not passionate about. It may be either complementary or only tactically usable: one is hardly able to force oneself to become good at something one doesn't really appreciate, but why not to use all that knowledge you have struggled to obtain? I, personally, could leverage my years at medical school and join a life science VC firm, but hey... I'd rather stay true to myself—I am no medic from any angle.

The same applies if you merely want to match yourself to a VC firm's investment profile, but are not passionate about any of the sectors they invest in: this will very quickly be spotted at the very first interview with you, so don't risk it. Generally speaking, if you feel like stretching any elements of your investor profile too far, just to be liked by a potential employer—resist!

The best way to approach the choice of your specializations, is to pick one or two sectors you are genuinely passionate about, and one or two sectors that are currently on the rise. The first choice will keep you deepening your knowledge in something you are already familiar with, and the second will make you learn something new, which is an integral, and possibly the most fun, part of being a venture investor.

Narrow Your Focus

Narrowing an investment focus is often a good thing, and can provide unexpected upsides. By narrowing your focus, you may look more professional, determined, and knowledgeable to your potential employers. Doing this doesn't necessarily mean that you should only invest in, for example, e-commerce mobile applications and nothing else. It may simply mean that you're looking for very specific things in a broad range of startups. How does this work?

We've already figured out when it's better to be a specialist, and when a generalist. Aside from your industry and sector investment focus, you should also determine your stage and geography preferences.

When it comes to the **investment stage**, investing in early-stage companies is very different from investing at later stages: you need different skills, competencies, and knowledge. Let me give you just a few examples.

To start with, you need to analyze different assets and datasets. Seed and early-stage companies don't have many assets besides the team, idea, and maybe intellectual property. They also won't have a robust financial history to analyze.

Furthermore, the risks at different stages of a company's development vary. At the early stage, the product and business model will be challenged: the product may not fly and the business model may be unsustainable. Later-stage companies have typically proved both of them, but may suffer from a deflating market and stagnating growth that is insufficient to keep the company afloat.

Another point to note, is that, although you can give some useful advice to first-time founders, you can't offer much to the CEOs of companies with hundreds of employees, unless you have experience managing a similar size company of your own.

Last on my list for this topic, which is by no means exhaustive, is a timeframe for an anticipated exit: you can't do much about it at an early stage, but investors actively participate in making M&A deals happen at later stages, which obviously requires a lot of connections, leverage, and negotiating experience.

Although one can learn almost all the necessary skills for investing at any stage, understanding your capabilities when applying for a job, will help you meet the expectations of your potential employer better, thereby increasing the odds of you getting the job.

Experienced VCs who have worked with companies at different stages of their lifecycle have the luxury of choosing the stage they prefer investing in. Early-stage companies typically appreciate more help, so working together with founders in times of uncertainty, may be a lot of fun. Other investors, however, prefer to stick to more mature companies due to them having a more structured environment.

Let's talk about **geographical investment preferences** now. One of the most popular questions I regularly receive, is whether a young investment professional can move to the United States from another country and find a job in venture capital. Besides the fact that VC firms in the US typically do not sponsor visas and relocation, they also expect new hires to understand the local market perfectly. There is no shortage of candidates for VC jobs in the United States, so unless you have a unique superpower, the odds of getting such a job are against you. Nevertheless, I have seen a couple of cases like this.

The thing is that the United States, as a market, is huge, and many companies from around the world want to target it either as a primary market, or right after they have tested their abilities in their motherland. So it's no wonder that some aspiring investors learn as much as they can about the US market, even from abroad.

However, don't disregard other countries as well. China is another market that is currently booming at an astonishing speed. India—although not talked about much yet—is the next huge market to target. Latin America has been in the news for quite a while, but its entrepreneurial ecosystem is still in its infancy.

Aside from focusing on the US market, think how you can leverage your knowledge of other countries. Even if your future employer never invests in these markets, you can still benefit from the knowledge you have gained. For example, you can focus on educating local entrepreneurs and building your social media profile on this mission. Or you could write for the local media in your mother tongue. Venture capital is a business of opportunities, and that may as well be applied to the job search. Anything that can enrich your profile and bring value to the venture capital firm you work for, must not be forgotten.

Other than these focuses, some venture capital funds can be very creative and also pick some sort of **specialty based on their expertise**. Let me list only a few of these: healthtech products and services created for women and children, startups directed at reducing waste, or startups that can improve or replace government work. As you can see, these are very narrow focuses, however a lot of very different startups can fall into each of them: SaaS, hardware, e-commerce, etc. Are you beginning to see how a narrow focus can broaden your opportunities?

A narrow focus also doesn't mean you are prohibited from investing in companies that aren't described in your investment profile. It's totally common to say that one invests in "SaaS (in general) with a focus on... something (in particular)". It only means that you have certain preferences and proactively look for specific solutions, but are open to the rest of the sectors as well.

The purpose of all of this work is to help you design your tagline— a **high-level description** of companies or entrepreneurs you are looking for. For example, Ashton Kutcher says that he doesn't invest in any specific sector, stage, or metrics. Instead, he says: "I'm proactively funding brilliant people, trying to solve hard problems". Andreessen Horowitz "backs bold entrepreneurs building the future through technology". Sequoia Capital "helps the daring build legendary companies." Although these three examples sound very similar, you can feel that Kutcher is more impact-oriented, Andreessen Horowitz is nerdy and appreciate technology the most, and Sequoia is passionate about building great companies (which may not necessarily be very impactful or built on some outstanding technology, for instance). This is merely a case of semantics though, because most people don't look that deep (but hey, these three firms all said kinda the same thing, just differently, and they seem to be perfectly differentiated from each other). However, it is what makes you unique—particularly in the way that it relates to you as a potential employee.

Like I said before—and I cannot emphasize this enough—your investment profile should be carefully crafted, not only to make it very clear and genuine, but also to be flexible, so that you can change it when you are ready. The right way to think about your investor profile is that it should actually open new doors and opportunities for you. Therefore, every word you use should make others want to work with you—whether they are your potential employers, co-investors, entrepreneurs, or anyone else that may be of value.

ASSIGNMENT 2

Creating an investor profile is an important part of the program. Based on their level of knowledge of venture investing, I direct my coachees to certain sources, to obtain additional information on the subjects necessary for this exercise. It also requires a lot of self-reflection to truly understand one's motives and drives, and to determine one's current interests and passions. The second chapter accurately reflects each step we take when creating an investor profile, so follow these questions and exercises:

1. How would you rank the main motives of a venture investor that we discussed?
2. Using the worksheet, list your main drives and personal returns from the list, add your own suggestions, and rank them from most important to you, to least.
3. What type of investor would you like to become: a traditional venture capital fund manager, an angel investor, or a corporate investor?
4. Determine your investment focus: industry or sector, geography, stage, and entrepreneurial profile, etc.
5. Design your mission statement (or vision statement).

CHAPTER 3

DRAFTING YOUR CAREER PATH

What Venture Capitalists Do Every Day

Venture capital deal-making is based on a lot of communication with other people: entrepreneurs, limited partners, corporations, and other investors. Although it may sound counterintuitive, not only limited partners, but also entrepreneurs are your clients to serve. Because these are the main fuel that a venture capital business runs on, you could call it a service business.

I know some venture capitalists who strongly disagree with this notion, and all of them were or are currently at the top of the food chain in the industry: they are either some of the first VCs in Silicon Valley or belong to top VC firms in the market today. Because they once dictated, or still do dictate, the rules of the game and are being worshipped, they seldomly serve anyone.

Although VCs pay for entrepreneurs' business experiments, that in no way allows investors to treat them as inferior. Entrepreneurs are VCs' major clients. They are the people who VCs earn their returns from, and who will introduce other successful entrepreneurs to their favorite investors. So I strongly believe that even the mammoths of the venture capital industry should respect entrepreneurs as equals, regardless of their prior experience.

Due to there being an enormous amount of venture dollars in the market, and strong competition for a few brilliant companies, all other venture investors need to have something else to offer, aside from merely a check. Here is where additional expertise, personal charm, and "more than meets the eye" come into play, giving you the chance of being chosen among dozens of other potential investors.

"When I meet an entrepreneur who's considering partnering with us, I tell her that I'm not a founder's friend. I am a founder's business partner. My job is to do everything in my power to help make her and her company enormously successful. I'll work 24/7 to help realize the full potential of her idea. We will likely become good friends over time."

Doug Leone, Partner at Sequoia

The most promising startups that see a line of investors behind the door with their checks ready, have the luxury of choice, and interpersonal relationship chemistry will affect their choice significantly. So if you aren't one of the most successful venture capitalists and also don't like dealing with people, you should probably consider another job.

Depending on the stage of a venture fund's lifecycle, its partners spend varying amounts of time meeting all the people mentioned above and others. The daily job will be different for junior staff, of course, but since we'll cover the responsibilities of all main team players in the next section, let's focus on a general partner's day for now.

When it comes to meeting **entrepreneurs**, it's pitches, pitches, pitches at the start of a fund's investment period, and advising, advising, advising, later. The more companies in a fund's portfolio, the more time partners spend on helping them with their operations.

Other investors and partners (like angel investors or universities) of a venture firm, take the next piece of the time distribution pie. A VC's network is the best channel for deal-sourcing, because the startups presented by VC peers have already gone through their filters, and the odds of finding a worthy company are higher. Smaller and younger venture funds also source deals from other resources—from attending different pitch events, to making cold calls. In larger funds, associates do this job, but since entrepreneurs are equals to VCs, there is nothing wrong with a general partner reaching out to a potential portfolio company themselves.

Speaking of pitching **events**… this also falls into the category of networking. You never know where and when you'll come across the next big thing or meet a potential acquirer of your portfolio company. Although only attending events and using all the opportunities available to source deals is good, optimizing your networking time and building your way up to becoming a speaker or a judge, gives you better visibility so that entrepreneurs can find you themselves. Some partners focus on marketing, become spokespersons for their funds, and spend significant time speaking and judging, blogging, and giving interviews.

> *"You will not find me at conferences. I do not write blog posts. I avoid "humble" self-promotion on Twitter and Facebook. It's not about me. This behavior is part focus and part allergy. Don't get me wrong—I love working with people. That is what gets me up in the morning. It is what I do. However, anything that is more than a degree away from supporting a company or founder, feels like misused time."*
>
> Bryan Schreier, Partner at Sequoia

Finally, **limited partners** are critically important clients of venture investors because they're the main source of money in a current fund, and possibly, in the next funds—years from now. It goes without saying that if your current limited partners are satisfied with your job, they'll stay with you in the future and bring other limited partners with them. Typically, a venture fund sends quarterly and annual reports to the limited partners, however more and more LPs are willing to take a proactive position these days, which means they'll communicate with general partners more frequently on an informal basis.

Chris Arsenault, Managing Partner of iNovia Capital, suggested the following breakdown of his working day:

Image 3.1. Breakdown of a working day of a venture investor.
Source: Chris Arsenault.

As I've mentioned before, everyday tasks may differ depending on the stage of a venture fund, which is why it's tricky to judge the time allocation by just one graph. In this diagram, you can see that Chris spends the least amount of time on listening to pitches, and most of his time on helping his portfolio companies. This may mean that their fund has invested a bigger portion of their reserves already. He is lucky to spend only a little time on fund management itself, even including communication with limited partners in this piece of the pie. Fund management consists of legal and financial work, managing the team, and reporting. Larger firms have the relevant staff for each of these responsibilities, but if you're a partner at a smaller firm, most of these tasks are on you, even if you outsource some of them. It will, of course, take much more of your working time than 15%.

What else is missing in this diagram? Correct... due diligence and financial modelling. Again, the partners of larger venture firms rarely do this—it's a job done by analysts and/or associates. Whoever is responsible for sourcing and evaluating deals, will spend more time on sourcing and conducting preliminary due diligence, less time on more accurate due diligence (because a few startups will be considered for investment), and then a fair amount of time on financial modelling. Generally, early-stage firms tend to do more sourcing and preliminary due diligence (financial modeling makes little sense for early-stage pre-revenue companies), while late-stage firms do more accurate due diligence, financial modeling, and deal execution work.

Now, don't forget another important job—deal closing. This doesn't fall into the "pitching" slice, nor into the "helping portfolio companies" slice. Nevertheless, executing deals sometimes takes months of negotiations, and that doesn't include due diligence and drafting legal documents. The timing for this responsibility depends greatly on the stage of the company that a fund is backing: the more mature a company is, the more other investors are involved, the longer it may take to close the deal. Although lawyers are always involved in this process, it never happens without the partners or principals of the fund.

In a study called "How Do Venture Capitalists Make Decisions" by Gompers P., Gornall W., Kaplan S. & Strebulaev (2016), the venture capitalists surveyed, reported that they work about 55 hours per week. Out of that time, they spend an average of 22 hours networking and sourcing deals, and an average of 18 hours working with portfolio companies. The study also reported that the average deal takes 83 days to close, and the average firm spends 118 hours on due diligence over that period, including reference calls: late-stage firms call 13 references, on average, while early-stage firms make an average of only 8 calls. The study also revealed that the deal period and time spent on due diligence are shorter for early-stage, IT, and California firms, and longer for late-stage, healthcare, and non-California firms.

As you can see, there is no one correct diagram that can reflect a VC's daily duties accurately, which is why I draw your attention to all the possible tasks you would have to dedicate your time to, including proper planning of the team's and your personal schedules.

So what do we have after all?

Pretty much irregular working hours in a likely 60-hour working week, but with flexible enough weekends. The working schedule of a venture capitalist changes significantly depending on whether the fund is in the "fundraising", "deal sourcing", or "deal execution" mode, and is busiest when closing deals.

Do You Have What It Takes To Work At A VC Firm?

Let's face it, in order to become a general partner, one needs to have so many skills and a lot of experience and knowledge, that identifying and listing them all would be an academic study in itself. Nevertheless, I decided to try and list the requirements for VC investment professionals of different levels, based on the frequency of such requirements mentioned in the VC job descriptions from January through July 2018 (600+ job descriptions). You can download this list from my website.

When it comes to titles, there is no solid nomenclature in venture capital, e.g. an associate can be the most junior position in one firm, but in others, an associate can take observer board seats in portfolio companies like partners do. Likewise, the "venture partner" title may belong to a partner-emeritus who founded the venture firm decades ago, still brings in deals, but chooses not to oversee the entire deal-making process... or it could belong to a person who may be too young to become a full-time partner at a venture firm and "outsources" as a venture partner instead. As a result of this, keep in mind that there may be shifts in the sets of "must-haves" for any positions you apply for.

I will describe all of the most common positions at venture firms in this chapter, but let me start with a short questionnaire that lists some of the relevant skills, experience, and knowledge requirements that will help you get into venture capital in such positions as "analyst" or "associate", or similar ranks in corporate venture capital, such as "business development manager" (typically, the same work that associates do).

Part 1

Mark each function that you are comfortable with:

- Search and collect data
- Organize data
- Analyze data
- Report results

Mark each hard skill that you have:

- Reading financial statements
- Building data models
- Working in Excel, Word, and PowerPoint (or substitutes)

Mark each soft skill that you have:

- Self-motivation
- Patience
- Critical thinking
- Problem solving abilities
- Attention to detail
- Planning
- Self-discipline
- Multi-tasking
- Communication
- Flexibility
- Work ethic

The more check-marks you have, the more likely that you will be considered for an analyst position.

Part 2

Now, let's see what associates must be able to do.

Mark each function that you are comfortable with:

- Searching for investment opportunities
- Identifying potential investments
- Conducting due diligence
- Evaluating investment opportunities
- Presenting potential investments to senior management

Mark each hard skill that you have:

- Business modeling
- Budgeting
- Maintaining databases

Mark each soft skill that you have:

- Intellectual curiosity
- Adaptability
- Strong oral and written skills
- Decision-making skills
- Interpersonal skill sets
- Teamwork
- Quick learning abilities
- Willingness to take initiative
- Ability to work under pressure

The check-marks in this part are relevant for an associate position. To get it, however, you need to have as many check-marks as possible in both Part 1 and Part 2.

As previously said, an associate position can be ranked differently from firm to firm. At venture firms that don't have analyst positions, the responsibilities of an analyst are typically performed by associates.

Associates with venture firms that have analyst positions, often perform some of the job functions of partners. To level up, you'll also need to possess the following skills, knowledge, and experience, in addition to all of those listed above:

- Project management
- Negotiating
- Risk management
- Transactional experience (legal, financial)
- Leadership
- Mentoring
- Conflict resolution
- Team building
- Technological and/or entrepreneurial background
- Academic strength
- Strong network (industry connections)
- Marketing (social media presence)
- Creativity

What about education? As far as skills and experience are concerned, education is irrelevant.

"When I was contemplating going to business school after LinkExchange was sold to Microsoft, Michael Moritz (who graduated from Wharton, but never includes it in his bio) told me, "You learn more in three months at a startup than at business school." I've been working at or with startups ever since."

Alfred Lin, Partner at Sequoia

Of course, you will see many VC job openings where Ivy League schools or MBAs are mentioned among other requirements. In practice, however, that only really matters when there is little else to showcase. If a venture firm is hiring interns, an MBA or some other indicator of education will always be present, because the chances that applicants will be like a blank sheet of paper are high. However, if you have experience that is valuable for an open position—rejecting you for the sole reason that you don't have a pedigree, would be an oversight.

Keep in mind that some of the requirements for candidates of all levels, are simply inherited from the early days of venture capital. First it was semiconductors and hardware, and innovations were born at universities. Their network was the only in existence, so belonging to it was critical. Then it was "software eats the world" and the era of the apps—this is how we got coding and engineering as must-haves. Most recently, it was the gig economy, and now it's blockchain. Innovations have become more diverse, and so have venture investors. With all due respect to traditions, it's your unique qualities and different views that matter.

The Hierarchy At A Venture Capital Firm

Venture fund teams can be structured differently depending on their size and the investment stages they focus on. There is also no standard title nomenclature or strict job leveling at venture firms, but, in general, the hierarchy looks like this:

Partner Level
General or Managing Partner, Junior Partner or Principal, functional Partners (i.e. marketing or talent partners, etc.), Venture Partner.

Junior Level
Associate or Venture Fellow, Analyst, Intern.

Venture capital is one of the very few industries with an inverted pyramid structure, where you may find more partners than analysts or associates in any given venture firm.

Some other positions external to the firm's hierarchy include: Officer, Entrepreneur-in-Residence, Marketing Manager, Portfolio Support Manager, Admin, Scout, and other typical business positions.

Managing Partner or General Partner

Many venture firms call them 'partners', while some call them 'managing partners' or 'managing directors' (unless this title belongs to an employee hired specifically to run the firm). You can also see such titles as 'founding partner' or 'co-founding partner'. These are the true GPs of the firm who may also have their names on the door. General partners raise the money for the fund, but also contribute a small amount of their own money to it. They make the final decisions on which companies to invest in, and take seats on boards. They hold the main stakes in the anticipated carried interest and have the highest compensation at a firm. At large firms, however, some general partners tend to be less involved in the daily deal-making, and are more focused on high-level tasks such as identifying key sectors to invest in, giving the green light for investments and exits, networking at a high level, representing the overall firm, raising money for the next fund, and communicating performance to investors.

Junior Partner or Principal

These two titles are often used at larger venture funds and are only slightly different. There's a need every few years to bring in one, or more, new partners to refresh a venture team. Often, experienced VCs within the firm, recruit successful entrepreneurs or operation managers from their network. Alternatively, they may promote younger professionals from within the firm.

For the sake of motivation, many firms sometimes call them 'partners' or even 'investment partners', though they often do not vote on investment committees, let alone make investment decisions.

Junior Partners are typically expected to be a source of high-quality deals and can work full or part time. Principals (can be also called 'managing directors') are usually full-time employees who are expected to perform such additional functions as investor relations, negotiating partnerships for portfolio companies, managing a fund's community, and the finance and legals of the fund itself, etc.

Junior Partners and Principals at most firms have the authority to lead their own investments and sit on boards, however, they rarely have a vote on deals, and only about half of them have direct fund carry, commonly being compensated from the overall performance of the fund.

Moving from Principal or Junior Partner to a Partner is simply a matter of making some successful investments. Within big firms, Principals are promoted from Associate positions (I'll describe below). It is rare to join a VC firm at the Principal level, and generally takes 2-4 years to go from Senior Associate to Principal.

"In my view, the firms that use the title "Partner" loosely and almost promiscuously, are doing a disservice to entrepreneurs. They should be more transparent about how the process works in their firm, and if part of that process is to get through some gatekeepers, then that's okay too."
Manu Kumar, a geek turned entrepreneur turned investor and the founder of K9 Ventures

Venture Partner

A Venture Partner is a person brought into the VC firm to facilitate and manage investments, but is not, or not yet, a full and permanent member of the partnership. The term "Venture Partner" can have several different meanings depending on the firm in which it is used. Some venture firms use this title instead of "Junior Partner", and other firms use this title for retired (either voluntarily or involuntarily) Managing Directors (MDs) or GPs. Also, this title can be used for someone who doesn't want the responsibility of being an MD, or only intends to be at the VC for a specific period of time. In other words, this title can be assigned to a position "on the way up," "on the way down", "on the way out", or "just hanging out for a while". It is definitely the most confusing of all the industry participants, since it's never completely clear what legal and decision-making role they play at a fund. They may or may not have a salary, and if they do, the overall compensation is often mainly based on the success of those very companies they added to the fund's portfolio, unless they become legitimate managing partners. Anyone can have this title—from young professionals trying to make their way up the ladder, to seasoned company executives becoming first-time investors.

Functional Partner

Recently, a new type of Partner has appeared in the industry—the partner that operates in a functional role such as Marketing, Talent, or Operations. These titles are pretty much equal to commonly known executive-level positions such as: Chief

Marketing Officer, Chief Human Resources Officer, and Chief Operating Officer. These partners do not typically contribute to the fund and fully focus on their specific functions, however, they can be motivated by bonuses coming from carry, therefore, their 'Partner' titles can be explained by that.

Being a bit opinionated, it would be fair to say that these titles are often granted to women in an attempt to increase the ratio of women in partner positions at VC firms. This is, of course, misleading when it comes to the diversity of investment team members who actually take part in investment decisions.

Associate

Associates are usually gatekeepers for the top managers of a venture firm. Their primary functions are to source new deals and support existing investments, doing all the boring work—from cold calls to crunching numbers. In large firms, many associates have an 'analyst' position below them. Associates also get the chance to network with entrepreneurs and watch the trends within their firm's industry focus. At a few firms, this is a partner-track position, but in most instances, it is not. Big firms can have two levels of this position: associate and senior associate—depending on their level of education, i.e. pre-MBA or business school graduates respectively. Traditionally, associates are usually ex-bankers, consultants, investment professionals (i.e. private equity or other VC funds) or operational leaders with three to five years of experience, sometimes with an MBA or a PhD. However, many top tier venture funds also hire engineers, or operations or product managers with strong technical backgrounds (e.g. software engineer after three years at Google, or an analytics PM with four years of experience at Apple or Facebook).

Oftentimes, VC firms hire associates for two years only, meaning there is rarely an opportunity for internal advancement at a VC firm. Both senior and junior associates do not usually have the authority to lead investments and sit on boards, thus, they often join a startup in an operating role or go to business school after their contract expires. However, in some firms, an associate position can lead to a principal position or even have some of its functions as noted above.

Analyst

Analysts come to VC firms directly out of college. If they find themselves at larger firms answering to associates, they get the most boring part in venture capital working as "number crunching deal monkeys" (© Brad Feld). Analysts screen business plans before passing them to associates and senior staff, and conduct due diligence or research on promising industries and entrepreneurs. A background in finance and some outstanding college internship or business experience, have been known as the must-haves. However, other quantitative backgrounds such as engineering, math, economics, or statistics, are also strong backgrounds for the typical analyst roles. Analysts can be promoted to the associate level after a few years, but many of them choose to do an MBA or go the entrepreneurship route, founding their own businesses. Now, let's discuss each level in details and find the best fit for you.

Choosing An Entry-Level Position: Analysts & Associates

The analyst and associate positions at venture capital firms are regarded as entry-level positions, and are often interchangeable in the job market. Let's try to distinguish between them in order to increase your chances of getting hired.

Firstly, let's accept the fact that every investment professional at a venture capital firm—from analyst to partner emeritus—is expected to bring in prospective deals. So do not be confused when you read the term "deal-sourcing" in the job description for an analyst position, especially for smaller venture funds. If a large venture fund is hiring an analyst, nobody will actually bet on the analyst's suggestions. So, for the sake of distinguishing between these two positions, let's keep in mind that deal-sourcing for an analyst at a large VC firm is facultative, while for an associate it's one of the main job functions.

Another difference is that analysts are rarely supposed to communicate with potential portfolio companies beyond their traction, market, and financial data gathered for an analysis, while associates can participate all the way along the deal-making process and monitor the startups after that.

As previously said, some venture capital firms have people in both positions, in which case the associate is deemed senior to the analyst. Other firms only have one of them, which is typically the associate, and combines the responsibilities of both positions. Depending on the actual functions assigned to these positions, they can be ranked differently from firm to firm. In larger firms, associates do all of the jobs that partners do, and can even take observer board seats in portfolio companies. Such a ranking depends on whether this position is on the "partner track" or not, meaning that a person hired for this position can be considered for promotion to the partner position over time. When hiring, venture capital firms specify if a position is on the partner track, so if the job description doesn't say anything about it, feel free to ask. There may also be other hints about the firm's plans for you.

For example, if a venture capital firm is looking for a "pre-MBA" analyst or associate, it will likely offer a 2–3 year job contract, so that the employee can move on to business school or another employer.

Pre-MBA candidates are typically expected to have bachelor's degrees in mathematics, statistics, finance, economics, or accounting. Because VC firms focus on specific sectors, they sometimes pursue candidates with the relevant experience, and can ignore the absence of prior finance or venture capital background, e.g. a venture capital firm focused on mobile solutions may hire a developer who founded a mobile app startup.

If the job description mentions "post-MBA", it means that the VC firm is looking for a long-term team player who can potentially be considered for the partner track.

Why don't all associates eventually become partners? Because there just aren't enough potential partner positions, especially in smaller firms, and you need to understand this situation clearly, in order to avoid disappointment.

Now that you understand the general differences between the positions, let's try to determine which one is a better fit for you.

If you don't have any operational experience running a company, have no sectoral expertise, you haven't built your profile in the venture capital industry, or have no track record, then the most junior role as an analyst is your starting point. What is expected from you is, typically, analysis, so be prepared to be a "number crunching deal monkey". If the jobs of analyst and associate are combined, then deal-sourcing and communication with startups will also be required. The good news is that you can start doing all of this right now while looking for a job. Not only can you practice the skills you'll be expected to have, which will help you to stand out among other young candidates like yourself, but you will be able to enrich your application in order to catch the attention of your potential employer.

If you're looking for an associate position, then do-it-yourself training may not be enough. Whether we're talking about a combined associate/analyst position, or that of an associate with a well-established, big venture capital firm, there are two main jobs that they have to perform with little or no training: deal-sourcing and screening deals.

Deal-sourcing happens on the front lines by cold calling, at events, or during personal meetings in a startup's territory. Because there is a lot of venture capital money in the market and hundreds of other associates, you will be competing with other firms talking to pretty much every startup. This is why associates need to have a sales-like mentality, which will also be helpful when presenting prospective deals to the firm's partners.

As an associate, whether you have the help of an analyst or perform the analytical job yourself, you have to be able to conduct due diligence and financial modeling, understand whether a company is a good match for the venture capital firm's portfolio, and know how your VC team can boost its growth.

Depending on the venture capital firm's investment focus, the job functions of associates may differ too. VC firms that are focused on early-stage startups, do more deal-sourcing and very limited due diligence and modeling, because there is not enough data for a meaningful analysis. Venture capital firms that focus on later-stage financing do more of the traditional diligence, modeling, and execution, similar to a private equity firm.

Regardless of its junior level status, "venture capital associate" is a very desirable position because associates often do pretty much the same job as partners, meaning that they get their hands on almost the entire deal-making process. It's a valuable experience that opens the door to not only the same level position at larger VC firms, but also to higher ranks of the venture capital hierarchy. Some job descriptions state directly that they want to hire someone from another venture firm, so don't disregard associate job openings at smaller venture firms—experience with a small name VC fund is much more helpful than having no VC fund experience at all, if you're looking for a job in venture capital.

Read several job descriptions for both positions on www.vc.academy, to see what VC funds are looking for, and try to understand whether they have both analysts and associates on their team, or if the described position combines both jobs.

Grow Up To A Mid-Level Position: Principals and Directors

Mid-level positions include a variety of titles, e.g. Director, Principal, or Vice President, which may have various different annexes, such as Investment Director or Vice President, Business Development. The title of vice president is not common in traditional VC firms, but is typical in the corporate environment. For the sake of simplicity, let's agree to use "principal" as a code word for all mid-level positions.

If you read a job description for any such position, you will always find the following:

- Partner internally with other team members
- Develop strategic themes and actionable investment theses
- Leverage an existing deep external network to generate deal flow
- Evaluate and conduct due diligence on specific opportunities
- Communicate investment goals for each opportunity to the investment committee
- Negotiate, structure, and execute investments
- Prepare review materials and investment memos for governing bodies
- Oversee ongoing relationships with portfolio companies, including serving as a board member or board observer

This part should sound familiar to you, since it very much resembles what a higher-ranking associate would do. Indeed, people in mid-level positions do the same job as associates and partners. They are more trusted and autonomous than associates, but still don't sign checks, and don't get paid as much as the general partners do.

As previously mentioned, everybody in a venture capital firm is expected to bring deals to the table, so deep involvement in deal-sourcing and deal-making is natural for people in mid-level positions. However, there is a set of responsibilities that are typically assigned specifically to principals, because associates are typically not experienced enough to do them, and general partners don't want to do them (or don't have enough time for that). Such responsibilities generally relate to managing a venture fund as an enterprise, e.g.:

- Negotiate and communicate with partners, such as investment bankers
- Represent the fund at various industry events
- Lead internal events, such as portfolio reviews and presentations to stakeholders
- Develop group functions, capabilities, and processes
- Develop key internal people
- Monitor and manage the portfolio in order to achieve the fund's financial goals
- Prepare and present reports to senior management and limited partners
- Ensure compliance with procedures for all investment operations, policies, and activities

As you can see, this set of responsibilities requires operational experience, because a venture fund is as much a business as any startup, and all the general rules of running such a business apply to it too. You will still see almost all of the same requirements for analysts and associates, e.g. analytical or financial modelling skills, but they are magnified by the words "strong" or "outstanding". There will also be new additions to the list of requirements, such as:

- 5-10 years of relevant experience in venture capital or private equity
- A bachelor's degree in a related field
- Demonstrated experience in investment operations processes
- Consulting, corporate development, M&A, or VC experience is a plus
- The ability to make complex decisions
- Basic knowledge of relevant laws (depending on the sector and investment focus)

Principals also usually manage the lower rank employees—analysts, associates and other operational staff—and often play a leading role in the negotiation aspect and the transaction process. Principals can also be in charge of making portfolio companies run smoothly and will be on the board of a few portfolio companies.

All of these lists are by no means exhaustive—see examples of real VC mid-level position descriptions on www.vc.academy for: Director, Principal, and Vice President.

Principals get hired as partners-in-training, meaning that they may most definitely be on the partner track unless they don't want to. Many articles on the internet say that it is rare that one gets to be hired by a VC firm at this level. However, if a firm needs to headhunt a promising associate, the title of principal is the way to go (unless it's a big VC firm and an associate position is as valuable as a principal one), even if the set of responsibilities doesn't differ much from the associate's. If you start as an associate and build a strong track record, it'll take you 2-4 years to get the chance to be promoted from senior associate to principal.

The most important difference between the two positions, is that principals at most firms have the authority to lead their own investments, sit on boards, and some of them can even get a small percentage of the carry, in the event of success. However, they usually don't belong to the investment committee and can't vote on deals.

Overall, the principal level has a lot of influence in a venture fund and in the community, being the right hand to the partners of the fund.

Is There A Chance Of Becoming A Partner?

General partners are basically the founders of a fund. They are the people who raise all of the millions of dollars that the fund will need in order to exist and invest in startups. They do, however, also put their own money first, typically, in the amount of 1% of the total target size of the fund, in order to prove their serious intentions and monetary interest to the limited partners.

General partners are entitled to maximum proceeds from the venture fund's investments, but they also bear all the responsibility for its operations by holding the fiduciary and legal liabilities for the fund. Although there is no direct punishment for unfruitful investments, the poor performance of a venture fund is the main thing by which general partners are judged. If the fund doesn't return the investments to its limited partners, the chances that these general partners will raise another fund are low. Therefore, general partners bear the consequences of investment decisions, regardless of who brings the deals to the table.

General partners are often called "managing directors/partners" due to legal reasons—the term "general partner" equates to unlimited personal liability in the partnership paradigm, which lawyers always try to avoid. So, if you see the "managing director/partner" title, be aware that it may be a general partner of the firm, and feel free to refer to these persons as partners in verbal communications. That said, larger firms may simply hire people for the managing director/partner position without making them members of the investment team or giving them a share in the firm. In this case, it is a "principal" position that is merely called something different, which distinguishes partners with liabilities from hired partners who are not founders of the fund. Confusing, I know, but I warned you—venture capital firm hierarchy is very unstructured, so you'd better know all the options.

Partners and principals have very similar roles in a venture capital firm, but if there is one difference worth mentioning... partners are the most senior members of the firm and are the ultimate decision-makers.

If a firm has principals on its team, its partners will be less involved in the daily deal-making and operations, and will focus more on high-level tasks such as:

- Identifying key sectors to invest in
- Ultimate approval of investments and exits
- Holding board seats in some portfolio companies
- Networking at a high level
- Representing the overall firm
- Raising money for the firm (every five to seven years)
- Communicating performance to a fund's investors—limited partners.

Is there a chance of being hired as a partner at a venture capital firm? Yes, and there are several paths to choose from. However, you first need to understand why you want it and if you are suited to it. If you truly have what it takes to be a partner with a share in a venture capital firm, then raising your own fund may be a better option. Thinking that you would like to become a venture firm's partner because it seems like a very sexy title, is not the correct mindset to have. That kind of attitude will immediately be spotted by the managing partners of your potential employer.

However, luck is on your side these days, as many venture firms have created different functional partner titles, such as "operation partner", "talent partner", or even "design partner". There is, however, a catch. More often than not, these titles give you neither the power to sign checks, nor do they entitle you to carried interest. In most cases, this title is just a bonus that venture firms readily grant to talented professionals whom they are competing for against other potential employers.

This is a novelty in the industry, and brings even more confusion to the venture capital title nomenclature, which is already pretty messy. Everybody in the community knows the true value of such functional titles anyway, so don't plan to wave this title around in order to be hired as a managing partner with another VC fund. To understand what a functional partner does, please read the job description of a Deal Operations Partner at Andreessen Horowitz (http://bit.ly/a16z-job) and try to guess what other position we've already discussed that would fit this description.

If you genuinely think that you will have, or already do have, all of the necessary abilities and skills to be a valuable managing partner, then the best way to get there, aside from starting your own fund, is to get noticed. It bears repeating that the number of partners in any given venture capital firm is limited by the compensation. The carried interest is proportionally or disproportionally divided between all the partners, and every partner bites off a piece of carry from other partners. It's not a big concern if a venture firm manages large funds (Sequoia Capital has almost closed a new $12 billion venture fund, as at the date this book was published, so even just 1% of the management fee will make many partners happy), but partners of the majority of VC firms would prefer to work harder or hire more associates, rather than share their carried interest with new partners. Keep this in mind when pursuing partner positions, and learn about the partners, their leadership style, the fund's culture, and their future plans, before going to an interview. If there is no room for another partner, then don't waste anyone's time.

Because investment professionals on all levels do pretty much the same job, there must be something that can make someone stand out at the partner level and not at any of the lower steps. What might that be?

Becoming a partner is a long-term commitment, that ideally stretches beyond the current fund. Once you have joined a partner team, be ready to raise new funds with them. In order to do that, you will need to have a solid network of limited partners and/or have certain qualities to be able to raise money for these new funds. If you don't have wealthy people in your network who you could raise money from, you can still be of value by being "sold" to limited partners as a strong asset of the fund. For this, you will need the following:

- Domain experience (hopefully in a sector that the VC partners find exciting)
- A prior investing track record
- Strong access to high-quality deal flow
- Relationships with seasoned, all-star serial entrepreneurs
- The ability to help portfolio company founders with their biggest operational challenges
- Commercial judgement and the ability to find an exit
- A reputation in both the founder and investor communities
- Long-term vision and the ability to see opportunities and gaps in the market

This list isn't exhaustive, just like the other lists in this section. There are at least a dozen other requirements for each position when it comes to a job interview.

As you can see, all venture capital fund team members, from an analyst all the way up to the top where the general partners reside, perform more or less the same work functions. However, at every level, the complexity, significance, and responsibility for the outcomes that each position holds, increases considerably.

How Much A VC Is Worth

Now we know that investment professionals at all levels perform a massive amount of work, so let's do a reality check. Unless a venture capital firm has made several successful exits, the salaries and bonuses of everyone from the analysts to the managing partners, will be very average.

Let's briefly review a VC fund's economics so that you can understand what the compensation depends on.

Typically, a venture capital firm charges a 2% management fee annually from the total amount of capital commitments of its limited partners. All the salaries and office expenses of the firm are paid from this amount. There may be other types of expenses associated with deal-sourcing and deal-making, such as travel expenses or consulting fees, which VC firms usually reimburse separately from the capital commitments (on top of the 2%). However, because the competition for limited partners among venture capital firms is high, some firms are ready to pay for such expenses from their 2% management fee, in order to seem more attractive.

The salaries vary significantly from firm to firm and depend on many factors, e.g. the total size of the fund, the vintage of the fund, or the stage of the investment focus, etc. The annual base compensation of a managing partner of large funds such as Sequoia, is measured in seven figures. It's a lot, but it is possible and explainable, because this partner would more than likely be managing a couple of Sequoia funds of different vintages, and each of them would likely have hundreds of millions, or maybe even billions of dollars collectively under management. All of that is entirely due to the stunning success of Sequoia's investments. Millions in annual compensation is everyone's dream, but it is fair, considering the level of responsibility that the partner involved will have to manage, not to mention the importance of ensuring returns for the fund's investors. Quite honestly, Sequoia can justifiably afford it.

This is, however, an exceptional example. To keep things simple, let's consider a first-time early-stage venture fund located in the United States as a baseline. Based on the Compensation Survey Report and LinkedIn Salary data, the salaries of the investment professionals of such a fund would more than likely be on the lower end of the following ranges:

- Analyst – $52K–$150K
- Associate – $100K–$160K (An EIR's salary typically falls in the range of an associate's compensation)
- Principal – $120K–$180K (A venture partner's salary typically falls in the range of a principal's compensation, but also depends on the level of involvement—part-time venture partners may not receive a base salary at all)
- Partner – $130K–$300K

If we assume that such a fund has total capital commitments of $55M, then the 2% annual management fee would make only $1.1 million available every year for running the entire venture capital team, including all other expenses. A reasonable team for such a fund would consist of three managing partners, two associates, and two administrative employees—seven employees in total. The team's salaries alone would then almost exhaust the entire annual budget:

- 3 partners = $390K
- 2 associates = $200K
- 2 administrative employees = $160K

Don't forget that there are other expenses to be covered from the annual management fee, such as: the cost of office premises, e.g. rent; administrative expenses, e.g. reporting; sometimes there are expenses associated with deal-sourcing, e.g. travelling and tickets to industry events; and deal-making, e.g. advisory consulting, legal expenses, lunches, and dinners etc. All of this could easily cost up to $500K depending on the activity of the firm, which is expected to be pretty high in the first few years of operations.

Aside from the base salaries, each investment professional can be entitled to an annual bonus based on performance, but there is also another source of financial motivation called carried interest.

Carried interest or "carry" is a success fee paid to the venture capital firm from the profit that exceeds a specific return level. Let's keep it simple and say that the investors of our imaginary venture capital fund expect to return their $55M plus $5M on top of that—$60M in total. This means that if the venture firm exits all of its portfolio companies and earns $60M or less, it will not get any carry. However, if all the exits add up to $70M, for example, the venture firm will be entitled to 20% of the difference between the LPs' expectations and fund's returns, i.e. 20% of $10M. This will only mean a bonus of $2M to be shared between five investment professionals who have worked for 7–10 years. Do the math—that is not much! This also doesn't take into consideration the disproportionately shared carry between investment professionals of different levels.

Analysts are typically not entitled to carry. Associates are sometimes entitled to a percentage of the carry earned on investments in only those portfolio companies that they have worked with. Such a percentage falls in the range between 5% for junior associates and 22% for senior associates. Principals—if they are assigned to take board seats and observe certain companies— can expect the same carry. Venture partners' bonus compensation depends on how much time they spend at the firm and how deeply they are involved in day-to-day operations. They are either entitled to up to 25% of the carry earned on the investments they were involved with, or 1–5% of the total carry of the fund.

When a venture firm decides to motivate investment professionals with a percentage of the total carry earned by the fund, and not by a specific portfolio company, there is a catch. One or two portfolio companies may have successful exits, which can bring 2, 3, or 4 times the invested capital. However, if the rest of the portfolio fails, then the total return on the invested capital may be zero or even a negative amount. In this case, the venture capital firm is not entitled to any carry, and neither are its investment professionals. Obviously, managing partners would want to tie everyone to the overall fund's performance, so as not to owe anything from specific investments to other team members if the fund doesn't receive any carry at all.

Although the managing partners are the highest paid of all the team members, it's necessary to mention that they have an obligation that other members don't. That is their own capital contribution to the venture fund, which is typically required by limited partners. Managing partners of a venture firm are expected to put their own money into the fund in the amount of 1–3% of the total capital commitments, to prove that they have their own skin in the game.

Even if it's only 1% of a $55M fund's size, it would require each of the three managing partners of our imaginary venture firm to contribute almost $200K at the inception of the fund. Because not everybody might have this amount of money at hand, it is common practice for managing partners to contribute their relevant amount when a deal is being closed. In other words, every time the fund invests $1M in a startup, the managing partner puts $10,000 from their salaries on the table OR it may be proportionally subtracted from their salary.

By now, you are probably thinking that this job is poorly paid! That is often true for smaller first-time venture funds. The salaries at larger firms may also be very average, because larger firms may require more people on their teams. So how do venture capitalists exist at all?

Raising a new fund after the first one, and then raising another one... and another one every 3–5 years is what keeps venture capitalists afloat or makes them millionaires (and billionaires). That is why if you aim to become a partner of a venture fund, you truly need to understand the long-term perspective if you want to be satisfied with your job.

By becoming a venture investor—whether by raising a fund yourself or joining one as an employee—you're betting on the investments to make you money 8–12 years down the road. If your team succeeds, it is a good deal, but if you think of it in terms of short-term financial benefits, it may depress you.

What's the conclusion? Larger venture capital funds provide better salaries and bigger upsides overall, which is why everyone wants to work for them and not for small first-time firms. The latter, however, are easier to get into and provide a good start for one's career.

ASSIGNMENT 3

In the next step of the program, we analyse the candidacy of each coachee—we determine what knowledge and soft and hard skills they possess, and which of those they still need to work on. Using the worksheet with the professional requirements for VC jobs, mark those you already have up your sleeve, and those you still need to obtain. Then create a plan for yourself on how and when you are going to do so.

Another worksheet you will find on my website is a career plan template. Even though the uncertainty of venture capital affects career planning as well, it's important to map out your next several years in the industry, for several reasons. First—to be able to create an action plan. Second—to focus on relevant opportunities. Third—to not freak out if everything goes wrong.

RENATA GEORGE

CHAPTER 4

TUNING YOUR MINDSET

VCs Invest In Exits!

It is believed that venture investors back major innovations. It is also believed that they invest in the brilliant teams behind them. However, there are plenty of unfunded genius teams that create products and services that would change if not everyone's life, then at least the lives of a certain group of people. Why does that happen?

The truth is that it's not the product or team that venture investors invest in—it's the expected value of their investments that we are interested in. In other words, the main question a venture capitalist needs to answer when listening to a pitch is: **How big could the exit be?**

To illustrate this, let me give you just one of many examples (I find this one to be perfect). In his article for Atrium.co, Ashton Kutcher, the actor, angel investor, and co-founder of Sound Ventures, says: "A lot of venture funds try to optimize for returns. They run complex ratio economic models to determine what their diluted value will be at the end of the lifecycle of the optimal and non-optimal case of every given company. I don't do that. I just try to fund the best and brightest. I love working with the smartest and brightest people in the world on some of the hardest challenges. And oftentimes I make a return as a result of that."

You can imagine the audience sighing in awe.

But then Ashton continued and instantly ruined that awe: "I weigh investments based on two vectors:

1. Return
2. Happiness

The primary litmus I put on any investment is on behalf of my LPs. Will the capital have a potential of 6-10x returns in 5, 8, 10 years? If not, it's not going to be worth our time and money…"

This is the first explanatory example of **how** venture investors think. It's not an idea that drives our ultimate investment decision (because investors aren't necessarily creators who fall solely for ideas); and it's not even a revenue that makes us interested in a company (because it's entrepreneurs or businessmen who think in terms of a stable annual income). Venture investors think about selling their shares in a company before they have even invested in it! This is how twisted venture capital is!

We all want to differentiate ourselves from other venture investors. We want to show that founders mean the world to us. We also don't want them to know that although the aforementioned point is the absolute truth, it only becomes valid after we have calculated the odds of making money on their company. It doesn't matter if you do it in your mind or "run complex ratio economic models", understanding the ultimate goal of venture investing is critical whether you are applying for a job or pitching potential limited partners for your own fund. And you, of course, can invest in some breakthrough innovations and brilliant people along the way.

Whether you are an angel investor or a venture fund manager, you are investing for the sake of profit for yourself and/or your limited partners. The team, product, market, and everything else, are the factors that we consider, but they aren't truly the ultimate object of our investments. Truth be told, the venture capital model isn't perfect, and we will talk about that fact later.

Each potential investment is analysed, not only on its own, but also as a part of the portfolio of the fund. When the word "portfolio" isn't used as a collective noun for a webpage with a bunch of logos, it should be perceived as an economics term meaning "a grouping of financial assets" and an arithmetical framework for acquiring and managing such assets. As Chris Douvos, Managing Director of Venture Investment Associates, puts it: "The portfolio is your strategy in action".

In fact, many VCs would appreciate a pitch starting from: "Our company has N% chances of returning you M% of the invested capital over X number of years, and here is why…" But this analysis is a venture investor's job—not an entrepreneur's.

It might as well be an answer to the eternal question that all VCs get asked: 'What are you looking for in startups/founders?" We are looking for entrepreneurs who will provide our fund with a significant return. If they look like our ideal profile—great! If not, then we'll make an exception. Nothing personal—it's just business.

Imagine that you, as an individual, have several sources of income: your daily job, freelancing, regular royalties for your book, bank deposits, and stock in public companies, etc. Each of them requires a different amount of time and money for their creation and maintenance. Each of them earns you more or less money currently or potentially in the future. At some point, you start thinking that some of these sources of income are worth investing your resources in, but some aren't. For example, the bank rate on your deposit is so low, that you'd rather invest this money in Apple stock that grew almost 50% in 2017 alone. In both cases, you don't have to do anything to get a return on the same investment amount.

The same logic is fair in venture investing. Each startup will require more or less of the VC's money and time, so while listening to a pitch, we think about whether it's worth it at all, and if yes, then our next thought will be about how much of each we are ready to invest, and when.

Based on different probability laws, as well as the statistics of venture capital investing that have been collected over the years and venture fund economics, portfolio design determines how much money is allocated to each of the companies in that portfolio, and when you can spend it, in order to increase the chances of generating positive returns for the fund's limited partners. Therefore, to balance the cash flows and minimize the risks, you need to accurately and thoughtfully assemble the investment portfolio.

Let's see what a venture investment portfolio might look like.

Portfolio Returns by Number of Investments

Highly Concentrated Portfolio

#companies	15					
Outcome Type	**Freq**	**Return**	**Theoretical ROI**		**#Outcomes**	**Actual Fund ROI**
Loss	50%	0.0	0.00		7	0.00
Save	25%	0.5	0.13		3	0.10
Small Win	18%	3.0	0.54		2	0.40
Large Win	5%	15.0	0.75		0	0.00
Unicorn	2%	50.0	1.00		0	0.00
Total	100%		2.42			0.50

Modestly Concentrated Portfolio

#companies	30					
Outcome Type	**Freq**	**Return**	**Theoretical ROI**		**#Outcomes**	**Actual Fund ROI**
Loss	50%	0.0	0.00		15	0.00
Save	25%	0.5	0.13		7	0.12
Small Win	18%	3.0	0.54		5	0.50
Large Win	5%	15.0	0.75		1	0.50
Unicorn	2%	50.0	1.00		0	0.00
Total	100%		2.42			1.12

Highly Diversified Portfolio

#companies	100					
Outcome Type	**Freq**	**Return**	**Theoretical ROI**		**#Outcomes**	**Actual Fund ROI**
Loss	50%	0.0	0.00		50	0.00
Save	25%	0.5	0.13		25	0.13
Small Win	18%	3.0	0.54		18	0.54
Large Win	5%	15.0	0.75		5	0.75
Unicorn	2%	50.0	1.00		2	1.00
Total	100%		2.42			2.42

Source: Dave McClure

⟫ toptal

Image 4.1. Potential portfolio returns by number of investments.
Source: Dave McClure

Dave McClure, a founder and the former face of 500 Startups, advocates for large portfolios with dozens, or better yet, hundreds of companies. His main argument is that the probability of growing a unicorn in any given portfolio is fixed at 2%. Therefore, larger portfolios have simply better odds of finding such unicorns (as per his chart). We'll find out later in this chapter how true that is.

This is one way to approach portfolio construction, but not the only one. I'll guide you through the other options a bit later.

If you have always thought that a VC investor's portfolio is a collection of random companies chosen with one's gut, you have got it all wrong. Throughout this book I will try to show you a myriad of proof that most of the decisions that VC investors make, quantitative or qualitative, are—and should be—well-calculated. If that doesn't dispel the myth about gut feeling dominating the venture capital world for you, then it should at least manifest its minor role in the process.

Calculations keep happening in a VC's head subconsciously. The more experienced a venture investor is, the more automatic these calculations are, the more they resemble a "gut feeling". The latter and "the art of venture investing" have also had a reputation for being sacred knowledge due to a very different mindset compared to other types of investing, and the collective experience of each particular venture firm gained over the years of its existence.

The study we're going to talk about on the next pages, found that overall, VC firms as a class, appear to make decisions in a way that is inconsistent with the recommendations of finance theory. Nevertheless, it shows that venture investors still use financial models, just different ones from those that MBAs are taught. This study also reports strong statistics on the importance of different factors in deal-making and providing necessary returns, which proves that investment decisions based only on a gut feeling are an exception rather than a rule, after all.

Venture capital mindset is not obvious to anyone who hasn't been investing for a while, and the blog posts explaining it are rare and not the most popular on the web. This is why I wanted to explain the essence of it to anyone who is determined to build a career in venture capital. As any mindset that is different from yours, it is unnatural and may be difficult to grasp (we all recognize that there is a huge difference between the mindsets of women and men, for that matter). I believe in my readers and coachees, and I'm confident that you'll understand how the venture capital mindset works!

What Size Exit Is Big Enough?

We have figured out that the number one thing you should be thinking about when listening to a pitch, is a size of the potential exit. To determine this, an MBA would compare the pitching startup to similar companies in the market, their current valuations or, better yet, exits, if such have happened. Furthermore, one would probably build a portfolio model by ranking its companies from best to worst, according to their return in multiples of the dollar amounts invested and grouping the investments into three buckets:

- the bad companies that go to zero;
- the mediocre companies that do maybe 1x, and don't lose or gain much; and
- the great companies that return maybe 3-10x.

Although, every portfolio can fit this model, relying on it creates a certain mental framework, which may keep venture investors away from success.

Venture capital investing is very unconventional by definition, and relies on classic methods only rarely, in order to confirm an assumption or prove it wrong. The most successful venture capital funds have figured out an unorthodox formula for defining a target exit size, which sounds very simple and has nothing to do with finance theory: **each portfolio company should have the potential to return the entire fund at its exit**. By doing so, they remove their focus from the types of investments that almost never have outsized payoffs, and add focus to the types that sometimes do instead. This is another difference in the venture capital mindset.

This rule of thumb may seem very simple, as do many other things in venture capital, but don't be fooled. If venture investing were that easy, everybody would do it and make money. There is well-documented evidence that 90% of investors don't.

The approach of selecting companies—each of which could potentially return the entire fund size from its exit—is based on **the power law**. You are, of course, familiar with the 80/20 rule, also known as Pareto's principle, which states that, for many events, roughly 80% of the effects come from 20% of the causes. Pareto's principle follows the power law as well, and this is where it gets complicated.

The list of resources for this book, which you can find on my website, contains links to the best explanations of the power law in business and life, yet the power law concept takes some time to comprehend.

In very simple words, the power law implies that occurrences of greater magnitude are rare, while smaller occurrences are common. For example, in the case of wealth distribution, there are very few billionaires and a large percentage of the population holding very modest nest eggs, e.g. only 1% of people account for 50% of the world's wealth.

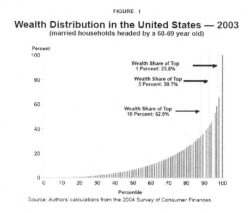

Image 4.2. Wealth distribution in the United States. Source: Eric Hofstad, Pinterest board

Another example: only a small number of companies pay the most income tax in the United States:

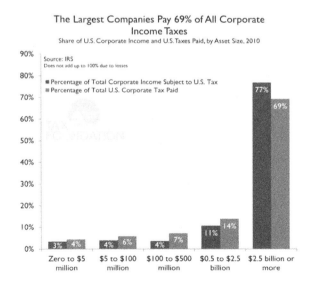

Image 4.3. Share of the US corporate income and US taxes paid by asset size, 2010. Source: IRS/Tax Foundation

Textbook example: the most destructive earthquakes are many times more powerful than all of the smaller earthquakes combined:

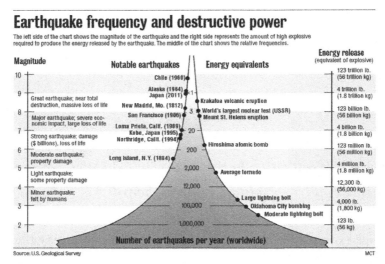

Image 4.4. Earthquake frequency and destructive power. Source: US Geological Survey

Even unicorn startups obey this law: the top 10 (out of 113) unicorns as of June 22, 2015, account for 46% of their total valuation, and the next 70 make up 45% thereof. There are still 33 more unicorns, but they are… you know… tiny unicorns.

Image 4.5. Unicorns by valuation, 2015. Source: CB Insights

This is the generally accepted curve of the power law:

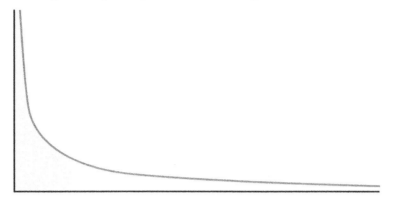

Image 4.6. The power law curve. Source: Wikipedia

Now that you literally have a clear picture of power law in your mind, let's dig deeper.

Generally, the relationship between two quantities may be linear, e.g. to double a cake's size, you need twice as much flour. If you have to drive a distance that is twice as far, it will take twice as long. Non-linear relationships are explained by the power law, and generally this means that you don't need twice as much of the original value to get twice the increase in some measurable characteristic. For example, an animal that's twice our size requires only about 75% more food than we do. This means that on a per-unit-of-size basis, larger animals are more energy efficient than smaller ones. As animals get bigger, the energy required to support each unit decreases. The simplest example of the law in action is a square: if you double the length of a side (say, from 2 to 4 inches) then the area will quadruple (from 4 to 16 inches squared).

The power law is named this way because exponential equations describe severely unequal distributions and is considered to be the law of the universe. Indeed, it defines our surroundings so completely that we usually don't even see it. For example, you have probably never thought that the very overused slogan "work smarter, not harder" comes from the power law. It only means that what you work on matters far, far more than how hard you work, even if you dedicate only 4 hours a week to it.

The power law is quite contrarian, and not surprisingly, it's the life principle of Peter Thiel, libertarian, founder of PayPal, first investor in Facebook, and an early investor in Palantir with an estimated net worth of $2.5 billion, who says: "We don't live in a normal world, we live under a power law". He talks in length about power law distribution in his book "Zero to one" and in the notes to his class "Startup" at Stanford. He even came up with the fundamental principle of how one might become a billionaire: "Indeed, the single most powerful pattern I have noticed is that successful people find value in unexpected places, and they do this by thinking about business from first principles instead of formulas".

By now, it should be quite obvious to you that venture capital is a clear manifestation of power law distributions, which can be applied from different angles. As Peter Thiel says: "In venture capital, where investors try to profit from exponential growth in early-stage companies, a few companies attain exponentially greater value than all others."

Indeed, venture capital is a fuel for companies to grow faster than they would without it. Fast growth provides an exponential increase in the value of a company (this explains significant changes in the valuation of a company from round to round, to a certain extent). In the venture capital world, a startup may not need a lot of money to show exponential growth. This is one dimension that the power law takes place in. Another dimension will show us that only a few such companies in one portfolio will be as valuable as all the rest combined—power law again.

The application of the power law also explains why smaller specialist funds often perform better than larger and/or younger generalist funds, which we discussed earlier in this book. The odds of finding one company that can be sold for half a billion and return a $50 million-fund are much better than finding a company that could return a billion-size fund. Of course, venture funds of a billion and above size, are typically created for later-stage investments, the model of which is somewhat different. Nevertheless, the law applies.

There is lot more to learn about power law distributions and their application in venture investing, so I decided to keep it short in this book and collect all other materials that would be instrumental to you when developing a power law (read: venture capital) mindset, on my website.

Failures Don't Matter

Nobody invests in losers deliberately. Nevertheless, the portfolio outline created by Dave McClure, shows that 50% of the investments in a portfolio of any size, become such. The fact that not every portfolio will have as many as half of its portfolio companies be failures, is as true as the fact that some portfolios may only have failures. In both cases, it only means that even among the brightest companies losses are inevitable, and anything with big potential has a high likelihood of failure. So don't you worry—even among those investments you see as promising, there will still be a considerable number of failures.

Every single company that looks like a winner may fail. The possibility of promising companies failing is equal to those of mediocre companies, especially in the early stages. In the case of a win, however, the former can return an entire fund, while the latter would only likely return a small portion thereof. Therefore, **it makes total sense to invest in only those companies that may be exited at a valuation of a billion US dollars or higher.**

I know it sounds like an ideal scenario, but the truth is that the top venture funds invest exactly according to this principle, which is also known as the Babe Ruth Effect.

Babe Ruth is widely considered to be one of the greatest baseball players of all time. What made him so famous was his batting ability, which allowed him to set multiple batting records. What is less well-known, however, is that Babe Ruth was also a prolific misser of the ball, and he struck out a lot. By "a lot" I mean that the "King of Strikeouts" was his nickname for many years. How can these two conflicting things be reconciled? Babe Ruth answers this question in his own words:

"How to hit home runs: I swing as hard as I can, and I try to swing right through the ball […] The harder you grip the bat, the more you can swing it through the ball, and the farther the ball will go. I swing big, with everything I've got. I hit big or I miss big. I like to live as big as I can."

We've already talked about the fact that most venture capital returns are driven by one, or a few, successful investments that produce outsized results. **The likelihood of a startup's failure is therefore less relevant to the aggregate performance of a portfolio than the potential magnitude of a successful outcome of an investment.**

In venture capital, everybody will have losers in their portfolio companies. Some investors will have winners. The questions are, how many winners will you have and how big will the exits be. Therefore, **a successful venture capitalist should look to invest in those companies that display the potential for truly outsized results, and not worry that they might fail.**

That is why failures don't matter.

However, the tolerance to failure doesn't come naturally to most people. This is yet another difference that separates venture investors from other... you know... normal people. Our brains are wired to avoid losses. Behavioral economists have famously demonstrated that people feel a lot worse about losses of a given size than they feel good about gains of the same size.

It gets worse with experience, because in most jobs and most industries, if something you do fails, that's a bad thing, and you might get fired. If you manufactured a car part that breaks, that means you screwed up. If you write a cover story for a newspaper that turns out to be untrue, you have a problem. Startups and venture investing don't quite work like this, however. If you take a normal, mature company to zero in a few years, your career is probably doomed, but if a startup doesn't make it, generally, that's just a normal risk.

Warren Buffett best described the venture strategy when he said: "...If significant risk exists in a single transaction, overall risk should be reduced by making that purchase one of many mutually-independent commitments. Thus, you may consciously purchase a risky investment—one that indeed has a significant possibility of causing loss or injury—if you believe that your gain, weighted for probabilities, considerably exceeds your loss, comparably weighted, and if you can commit to a number of similar, but unrelated opportunities. Most venture capitalists employ this strategy. Should you choose to pursue this course, you should adopt the outlook of the casino that owns a roulette wheel, which will want to see lots of action because it is favored by probabilities, but will refuse to accept a single, huge bet."

While he also agrees with Dave McClure's idea of investing in a big number of companies to increase the probability of success, not many venture funds follow this strategy. In the chart below, we can see that many funds tend to do up to only 20 investments per year, with larger funds (aside from a few outliers) focused on the lower end of the range.

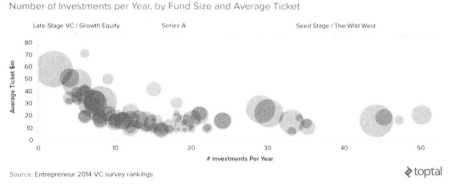

Image 4.7. Number of investments per year, by fund size and average ticket. Source: Entrepreneur 2014 VC survey rankings

There are a number of reasons why venture funds keep their portfolios relatively small, and the performance of accelerators with large portfolios is one of them. Data from several sources shows that the success rate of accelerator-funded companies to achieve a follow-on funding round, are significantly lower than the market average. Brian Solomon, a Forbes columnist, also calculated that: "Only 2% of companies emerging from the top 20 accelerators have a successful exit", which doesn't mean that those companies were unicorns or at least provided oversized returns. This implies that large portfolios of 100+ companies have below-average results, so why bother?

The truth is somewhere in the middle, and it also highly depends on the current market state. For example, Sequoia Capital had always said that they make 12 deals a year on average, until they started raising billion-size funds. At the time this book was published, Sequoia was the most active venture capital fund that did the biggest number of venture deals in the first half of 2018: the firm invested nearly $2.3 billion in 85 deals.

Larger funds mean bigger checks and/or more investments, but I bet that Sequoia will still shoot for the winners (if we only knew how they found 85 of them that fast!). They will of course have more failures, but they will also have more big wins. What's more important, is that they will need to have bigger big wins, in order to return those billions to their limited partners.

While there is an obvious trend of raising mega-funds of $1 billion and more, some seasoned venture investors still prefer to stay small. For example Fred Wilson of Union Square Ventures prefers to keep the fund as big as a quarter of a billion. He is known as one of the most thoughtful and successful investors and, of course, could raise more venture dollars per fund, but his decision to stay small is based on simple math.

In his blog, he wrote that for his fund to be successful, it needs to have at least two $1B exits. Although there are more than 250 private tech companies valued at $1 billion and more in the market, as of this moment, it's not the valuation, but the exits that matter: "If you do the math around our goal of returning the fund with our high impact companies, you will notice that we need these companies to exit at a billion dollars or more," he wrote. "Exit is the important word. Getting valued at a billion or more, does nothing for our model." After all, even after achieving a billion dollar valuation at some point, history knows companies that exited at a lower value or didn't exit at all, and ended up with down-rounds (new funds raised at a valuation lower than the previous investment round).

Do all VC funds invest in companies that can return their entire funds? Well, they try. However, they also remain realistic and have a plan "B", where they invest in companies that would provide at least oversized returns.

Make more big hits—not fewer misses. This is the strategy of those successful people who find value in unexpected places, according to Thiel. That is fair when applied to startups that looked like bad ideas in the beginning, but turned out to be great companies after all. Airbnb was famously passed on by many smart investors because people thought, "No one's going to rent out a room in their home to a stranger.

To see that value in something unknown, uncertain, or even bad, requires some deep insights. This is where narrow expertise and operating experience in specific sectors may come in handy. It's the intellectual curiosity (from chapter 2) that is invaluable in such a moment!

It may be impossible for an observer to recognize an opportunity that may turn a market upside down. Airbnb, Uber, and WeWork, are examples of that. The change they offered was somewhat contrary to the existing status quo. One needed to see the underlying trends in these industries and dig deeply into emerging technologies to recognize the potential. None of these companies were attractive as business plans. Quite the opposite—all of them have been capital intensive and only Airbnb has so far been profitable. What their first investors saw were the behavioral trends of millions of people around the world that would make these companies winners. That is why being a specialist investor on a personal level may increase your chances of success. A deep knowledge would help you "see the forest for the trees" when taking early risks. It's just the specialties that are in high demand that you need to choose correctly.

You now know that failure is a part of the venture capital game. However, I want to warn you that although failure should be tolerated, it should not become the norm. One cannot build long-term success on failures. Whether you are an entrepreneur or an investor, the number of times when you can fail and keep raising funds is limited. I've met con artists who recognized the high tolerance to failures in venture capital and were raising funds as both entrepreneurs and general partners, knowing upfront that they won't even be trying to succeed, because they would be forgiven anyway.

It is true that failure is a part of risk, and failing, in itself, does not mean that someone was stupid or screwed up. In venture capital, failure means that we tried. Nevertheless, it's the wins that make one a venture investor. Keep your eyes on the prize.

How To Spot A Winner

There is no formula for spotting a winner.

Any company can fail sooner or later.

The right question to ask is: "What if they win?"

How To Recognize Mediocre

It's become an anecdotal statistic that what initially seemed a bad idea, often becomes a winner, and those ideas that looked promising often end up in... the other basket. Therefore, be prepared for your favorite companies to underperform. If you think about a company as the one that will likely bring you a modest return, but definitely won't lose the money, the chances that it will become a failure, are high. To reduce the odds of adding losers to your portfolio, you need to be able to recognize mediocre companies, as they will likely be the ones that won't make it and will form that very loss.

Being a mediocre company, from the venture capital perspective, doesn't necessarily mean that the product or service of this company is bad, the team is incompetent, and the business won't fly. It may only mean that such a company can't provide sufficient returns for a venture fund that would make sense for its economics. Clearly, not every company or business idea fits the VC model nor is right for a venture capital. We don't hear much about such cases, but they are all over the market. Companies that earn enough to survive, but no one is willing to acquire them. Or companies that just become a lifestyle business that is satisfactory to the founders and employees, who are unwilling to sell it to anyone. There is a bunch of other scenarios to consider too.

Of course, the most successful venture investors somehow manage to find the diamonds in the rough, more often than others, but they also miss many. For example, Bessemer Partners, one of the top venture firms, has a list of companies they did not recognize as potential winners—with Apple, Facebook, and PayPal being among them. As you can see, that gut feeling that everybody is talking about, doesn't always work, even among the best of us. So how do VCs pick their bets?

In venture capital, especially in early-stage investing, there is nothing but uncertainty. You cannot find an answer to the question: "Will this company become a winner?". Many people think that the right way to approach it is to find reasons why the company may become a failure. The truth is that every company could become one—every single company. Even if it is founded and led by entrepreneurs with previous multi-billion exits in their sleeves! If success were an animal, it would be a zebra.

Image 4.8. Unicorn zebra. Copyright: Nongnapat Boonanunaka/gloly67/123RF.com

The question that you may have better odds of answering when assessing a startup is: **"What would it be like if it worked?"** In venture capital, one needs to put aside normal human risk-aversion and skepticism, and accept the equal probability of big success or big failure. This question would lead you to a set of smaller questions to answer, which will eventually lead you to a better understanding of how big the exit might be, if any, and this will help you to sort out the mediocre. **"How likely is it that the company will succeed?"** and **"How much can venture capital boost its growth?"** are some of the right questions to ask.

This success, of course, doesn't necessarily spread all the way to the exit. If you are a seed investor, you can only advance the company to the next stage. You may finance the product development, and the company may start growing, but if the growth doesn't pay for its existence yet and there are no other investors ready to fund the growing company, it is doomed.

There is a lot of math in this exercise, but portfolio construction and arithmetical calculations are outside of the scope of this book (follow my posts and newsletters to learn more). Let's explore the qualitative side of the subject, nevertheless.

Despite the fact that a lot has been said and written about how VCs make investment decisions, and this topic may seem exhausted, there is still no universal algorithm for assessing investment opportunities. You can find literally hundreds of articles, blog posts, and interviews on the web, with responses that have varying levels of detail. However, each of them will be different. So how are you supposed to know what's right for you? To make sense out of all the opinions you may have read, let's approach this subject from a scientific perspective.

A study published by The National Bureau of Economic Research, and conducted by academics from four universities, revealed a spectrum of approaches to the assessment of investment opportunities by 681 US venture capital firms. The surveyed firms were represented by 76% of the top 50 VC firms and all but one of the top 10 firms—the experience of these successful investors can definitely be trusted more than any other source. This is by far the most comprehensive study explaining how VCs make their investment decisions, and why. It also considers the fact that one size doesn't fit all, and different venture funds will have different assessment models. It is true for every other investment strategy and depends a lot on the investment stage, industry focus, and size of the fund. The study only compares venture capital funds focused on early-stage and later-stage investing, for the sake of simplicity.

The main question that the survey gives answers to, is: What are the factors that drive your investment selection, and how do you rank them?

Important Factors for Investment Selection		
Most Important Factors	Early Stage Percentage (%)	Late Stage Percentage (%)
Team	53	39
Business Model	7	19
Product/Technology	12	8
Market	7	11
Industry	6	4
Valuation	0	3
Ability to add value	2	2
Fit with the fund	13	13

Image 4.9. Factors for investment selection. Source: The National Bureau of Economic Research

As you can see, the top 5 factors are the same for both types of investors, however, they rank them differently. They are well-known, because VC funds' investment theses are often built on them and openly articulated in public. But what would an assessment of these factors tell us?

Let's consider only those startups that you would like to back. If all the above-mentioned factors are strong enough, you'll be in line with dozens of other investors. It's a mastery to not be scared away by weaknesses. If you like a startup at a pitch, but during a deeper assessment you discover one or several deficiencies, you need to find an answer to the question "**How likely is it that with my resources the company will eliminate the defects?**".

For example, if the team lacks an important player: "**How likely is it that with my resources the company can build the right team?**". Or if the product isn't impressive enough: "**How likely is it that with my resources the company can create an impressive product?**". This question is also very helpful when you have similar startups to choose from.

There is one more factor that hasn't been included in this research, but it turned out to be a leading factor of success in a study conducted by Bill Gross of Idealab. Looking at the reasons for success across a range of 200 startups, he concluded that timing accounted for 42% of the difference between success and failure. This was the most critical element, leaving the team, idea, business model, and funding, behind.

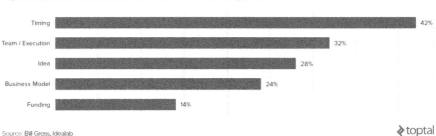

Image 4.10. Top 5 factors in success across more than 200 companies. Source: Bill Gross, Idealab

The venture capital industry has seen many examples where the timing was wrong for an idea. There's even a saying for that: "being early is the same as being wrong." Few of us know that SixDegrees.com was the original online social network, based on the idea that we're all six degrees/handshakes away from everyone else on Earth. It had high growth from its start in 1997, but people weren't ready to exchange their lives for a social network. The pet supplies online market, Pets.com, failed hard because it started at the top of the dotcom boom, while its twin-brother, Chewy.com, was acquired in 2017 for $3.35 billion in the largest e-commerce acquisition ever. Even Google Glasses didn't fly, although early-adopters went crazy about them several years ago. **Finding the right moment is only possible if you see a startup as an element of a larger system.** Those investors who can wait longer than venture capitalists, sometimes manage to: recognize great potential, even in companies that are too early for the market; back them; and then patiently wait until the timing is right.

With all this information collected, a venture investor then needs to make a decision whether the potential investment is worth their resources. Each portfolio company will require not just money, but also other intangible resources such as the time of the investment team, for instance. If the investment seems to be able to bring an outsized return, it's worth trying. However, if there is a doubt that this might be the case, most likely, this investment will eventually fall into the mediocre category.

The assessment of the likelihood of each potential investment becoming that very winner, involves dozens of other factors, including: stage, round size, and even who the co-investors are. You'll need to find where a company sits on the risk/reward curve and understand both the scale of the potential risk and the scale of the potential reward. Then, you'll need to build decision trees to take your bets. All of these are elements that form yet another system you need to work with in venture capital.

You can see that aside from quantitative, there is a lot of qualitative work, and a professional investment decision is never made without calculations. All this analysis should give you the average likelihood of the company's ability to return your entire fund over the years. However, that doesn't happen at your whim. If your gut, analysis, and forecast are favourable towards a company, you fund it and then work your arse off to advance it to the next stage. Then, in the next stage, you pray that its later-stage investors will be doing the same.

Don't Get Lost!

By the end of this chapter, I expect that you will be thinking: "Gosh, this all is so complex!". If so, I applaud you, because you get it! Venture investing is one of many types of investing practices. As Charles Thomas Munger, an American investor, businessman, philanthropist, and a vice chairman of Berkshire Hathaway (one of the ten most valuable companies in the world, and controlled by Warren Buffett) put it: "It's not supposed to be easy. Anyone who finds it easy, is stupid."

I also want you to remember the wisdom of another great person— John Kenneth Galbraith, also known as Ken Galbraith, a Canadian-born economist: "There is nothing reliable to be learned about making money. If there were, study would be intense and everyone with a positive IQ would be rich."

You may ask: "Does it make sense to try to learn venture investing then?" Let me explain why it does.

There are two factors to consider. One is that venture investing is much more fluid than any other investing practice—you need to constantly learn something new in order to stay on top of it. The other is that studies have found that older venture firms perform better than younger ones due to particular investing models that are created and adjusted over the years. There is not a single venture investor who knows everything about existing big hits, and you won't either. However, there is certain knowledge that can be learned, and this knowledge will become the foundation for building your venture investing mastery (a collection of such knowledge is what I've been working on during recent years). So yes, before you start practicing venture investing with confidence, there is a lot to be diligently studied.

Among all of the other skill and knowledge requirements listed in the previous chapter, I hope you noticed two of them that are combinations of skills and knowledge—system and critical thinking.

You are already familiar with the basics of the system thinking that can be applied to the venture capital industry in general, and to your job search in particular. You can now see why the investment portfolio of a venture fund is also a system. What's more important, however, is treating each pitching startup as a stand-alone system as well as part of a larger system. This approach will keep you from getting lost in the process of assessing it as a potential investment.

Uber is a strong example of how a startup was added as an element to a system that had never contained anything like this before. This small company affected the other elements of a large and very conservative system: traditional cab companies, their drivers, and customers. But it also brought new elements into it—new drivers and new customers, who both would never have become such without Uber as a new model. All of these actors changed the relationship or established new interconnections. And that's not all. Dozens of competitors appeared around the world, forcing governments and employee unions to take extreme measures to deal with an unexpected problem that was ruining the status quo. Finally, we've got the entire movement of uberization of other different services.

While Uber was fighting the inefficiencies of the traditional taxi business and winning, a competitor to all services alike appeared out of nowhere. Electric scooters are solving a problem that cannot be solved by cars of any size—avoiding traffic jams. Scooters, unlike cars, allow people to squeeze in between the cars and get from point A to point B much faster. Because millennials have been a big part of ride-hailing clientele and scooters have turned out to be a lot of fun, Uber and Lyft had only one way to deal with this sudden intruder—acquire one of the e-scooter companies to try to control the market, or at least have a seat at the table.

All of this happens within a system. I'm not sure that any of Uber or Lyft's first investors thought about this scenario when they backed the companies, but they definitely saw the magnitude with which they could affect the system of city transportation. Does it seem to you that one should be a futurist or at least a forecaster to imagine a scenario like this while listening to the pitch of a seed-stage startup of two co-founders?

If you are not Ray Kurzweil, a computer scientist, inventor, and futurist, now a director of engineering for Google, who has likely foreseen something like this, drawing a system around a startup is the best way to take a peek into the future. It can be done at any stage of a startup's lifecycle and can turn one's perspective literally upside down.

Read for yourself how Bill Gurley, a general partner at Benchmark, explains in his blog why Aswath Damodaran, a Professor of Finance at the Stern School of Business at New York University, where he teaches corporate finance and equity valuation, was far wrong with his estimate of Uber's market size and valuation. Gurley operates with different physical and non-physical system elements, such as pick-up times, payments, coverage density, trust, and safety. He is juggling with new use cases based on the relationship between elements of the system: rental cars, transportation of different family members (kids, elderlies, night-outs), as well as ride-sharing features. This is a great example of the system thinking.

It starts and includes all of the factors that we've discussed in this chapter. As a matter of fact, one should know when to stop, because some systems can be in a state of development indefinitely.

Whether you are at the analyst or partner level, analysing each of these factors separately wouldn't make sense. When you connect them to each other, however, and analyse the whole system, this is what an investment decision should be based on.

Important Factors for Investment Selection		
Most Important Factors	**Early Stage Percentage (%)**	**Late Stage Percentage (%)**
Team	53	39
Business Model	7	19
Product/Technology	12	8
Market	7	11
Industry	6	4
Valuation	0	3
Ability to add value	2	2
Fit with the fund	13	13

Image 4.11. Factors for investment selection. Source: The National Bureau of Economic Research

For example, the team is named as the most important factor for all VCs, regardless of the stage of the companies that they prefer investing at, but its significance varies. For early-stage investors, the team and the product/technology are the two most important factors, due to the likely lack of other assets. Later-stage investors have different priorities.

Obviously, when a company is mature, stability matters much more than anything else. Weak team members can be replaced with stronger hires, and a proven business model can keep a company afloat, at least for a while. The team weighs less for later-stage investors as a factor, but the business model is ranked second, being almost 3 times more important for later-stage investors than it is for their early-stage fellows. You get the point: it only makes sense if you see it as a whole.

To draw well-reasoned conclusions about a system when making an investment decision, wouldn't be possible without critical thinking. Unlike system thinking, it has an impressive history dating back to Socrates' teachings. He established the significance of raising vital questions and problems before we accept ideas as worthy of belief, and formulating them clearly and precisely—what we often call "asking the right questions". He proved the importance of:

- gathering and assessing relevant information
- closely examining reasoning and assumptions
- analyzing basic concepts and abstract ideas
- testing them against relevant criteria and standards
- tracing out implications of what is done as well

Haven't you read about these skills already? Correct—they were mentioned in job descriptions in one way or another.

A lot has been written about critical thinking and most of it is truly exciting. So as not to take your focus away from the subject of this book, I will deliberately stop here and finish this chapter with a poster found at a school. It's probably the best, yet simplest, framework for critical thinking that I've seen so far.

CRITICAL THINKING SKILLS

1 **Knowledge** **Identification** **and recall of information**	define fill in the list identify	label locate match memorize	name recall spell	state tell underline
	Who/what___? Where___? When___?		How___? Describe___? What is___?	
2 **Comprehension** **Organization and selection** **of facts and ideas**	convert describe explain	interpret paraphrase put in order	retell in your own words rewrite, restate	summarize trace translate
	Re-tell___ in your own words. What is the main idea of___?		What differences exist between___? Can you write a brief outline?	
3 **Application** **Use of facts, rules, and** **principles**	apply compute conclude construct	demonstrate determine draw find out	give example illustrate make operate	show solve state a rule use
	How is___ an example of___? How is___ related to___? Why is___ significant?		Do you know of another instance where___? Could this have happened in___?	
4 **Analysis** **Separating a whole into** **component parts**	analyze categorize classify compare	contrast debate deduct determine factors	diagram differentiate dissect distinguish	examine infer specify
	What are the parts or features of___? Classify___ according to___. Outline/diagram/web/map___.		How does___ compare/contrast with___? What evidence can you present for___?	
5 **Synthesis** **Combining ideas to form a** **new whole**	change combine compost construct create design	find an unusual way formulate generate invent originate plan	predict pretend produce rearrange reconstruct reorganize	revise suggest suppose visualize write
	What would you predict/infer from___? What ideas would you add to___? How would you create/design a new___?		What solutions would you suggest for___? What might happen if you combined___ with___?	
6 **Evaluation** **Developing opinions,** **judgements,or decisions**	appraise choose compare conclude	decide defend evaluate give your opinion	judge justify prioritize rank	rate select support value
	Do you agree that___? Explain. What do you think about___? What is most important?		Prioritize___ according to___? How would you decide about___? What criteria'd you use to assess_?	

Image 4.12. Critical thinking skills chart. Source: "Enokson"/flickr

ASSIGNMENT 4

The venture capital mindset can only be cultivated with training and practice. The good thing about it, is that you don't need to work for a venture capital firm to find the next unicorns. Start building your imaginary portfolio right away, using all available information to assess the startups. If someone is ready to work with you as an advisor, or in any other capacity—even better: you'll be able to know the company from within. After you finish Chapter 4, do the following exercises:

1. Find some examples of the power law in your life.
2. What big bets have you made so far?
3. What big bets would you need to make to achieve your current goals?
4. Find 2-3 early-stage startups that could be big and explain why. Your assessment will be very basic, so you don't need much of their internal data for it, but use as much public data about the relevant industries and markets as possible.
5. Choose a venture fund that you would like to work for—a smaller fund will work better for this exercise—and familiarize yourself with their portfolio. How do you think it will play out from the power law and Babe Ruth's standpoints?

CHAPTER 5

CLIMBING THROUGH THE WINDOW

Building Your Industry Presence

If you are reading this, then I haven't discouraged you from becoming a venture investor quite yet. By the time you reach this page, you should have already learned a lot! You now know where venture capital stands in the capital markets overall, how venture capital is different from private equity, and where in the world you can build your expertise and career. I believe you have figured out for yourself whether you need entrepreneurial experience or not, and that you have designed your investment profile by now. You should now understand more about the hierarchy at venture capital firms, and have a career plan for the next several years. Finally, you hopefully understand venture investors better as a result of becoming familiar with the concepts of the power law, making more big bets, and not worrying about failure. With all of this in mind, here comes another fun part of my coaching program—establishing an industry presence.

During my coaching program, we dedicate at least one session to each of the activities that I'll talk about further in this section of the chapter. Every one of them requires a bunch of basic knowledge and skills that are directly unrelated, but critical when looking for a job in venture capital. Some of this knowledge is common, while other parts of it may be obvious to you personally. I recognize that, but will nevertheless outline some of the very basic things, in order to give you a general framework with which to start. That said, there is a ton of information on each of these subjects that may be truly helpful, but is deliberately not included in the book. To access it, I invite you to use the knowledge base that you will find on my website www.renata.vc.

I prefer not to ignore this framework, but I also don't want to spend our precious time on developing each of the relevant skills during the program and on the pages of this book. My solution is a collection of relevant resources on my website, which you can use to obtain the skills and knowledge you may lack, at a self-paced speed.

Industry presence is an asset that cannot be created immediately, and can only be built over time. How long would that take? If you are serious about building your industry presence and are committed to dedicating enough time to it regularly, it would take a minimum of six months until you finally feel that Google knows enough about you. Depending on your career goals, it might take much longer. However, don't let this demoralize you. If you are new to the industry, you'll need time to get hired anyway, and that is unlikely to happen fast either. So, I always advise my coachees to not waste time, and to look for a VC job while working on their industry presence.

In the next section, I'll be talking in detail about actually applying for a VC job, but before that, there are some basic things you will need to take care of.

Social Media

Of course. As I've mentioned before, our hyperconnected world gives us a lot of opportunities (especially if we are looking for a job), but it also creates a lot of noise. Having a social media presence is, to a certain extent these days, necessary for a successful professional life. When you compete with hundreds of other bright people, you really want your profile to stand out. Generally, it is about the presentation: visual or textual.

For our purpose, you need to come up with a good bio and tagline, which should be based on the investor profile that you might have designed by now. Focus on the audience you would like to reach on social media: venture capitalists, entrepreneurs, reporters, etc. Think about what they pay attention to and what they may be interested in. Find the right words and images that will appeal to their interests, where applicable.

Next, in order to support your presentation, you will need to have at least some content on your social media timeline. Your potential employer will very likely look you up on Google and definitely scroll down a bit further than your profile picture. You will obviously need some content, creation of which may be more or less complex. If you haven't been an active user of social media, you can start with basics, such as sharing links to relevant posts from someone's blog, or articles from the industry media. Ideally, you need to start creating your own content, as that will speak for itself when your potential employer assesses you as a candidate. I will talk about this more, later.

It is important to review your older posts as well: you want to make sure that there is no compromising content left on your various profiles from your fraternity (or sorority) days. This often raises the question about whether it's right to suppress one's personality and real self on social media. The best way to approach this controversial issue is to use respect as a personal compass.

If a person's actions are a reflection of their true self, and they say something that may be publicly disrespectful towards others online, then this is evidence that this person may be equally as ignorant offline. Whether this might affect your job in venture capital or not, is for you to guess, but you will never know whether it has. Nobody will tell you that they didn't reply to the email with your resume, because they saw a picture on your Instagram page that turned them away. You might think that a male partner of a VC fund would appreciate a sexist joke on your Twitter feed, but you have no guarantee that the preliminary candidate screening will not be conducted by a woman!

This applies to any profession, of course, but because venture capital requires that you communicate with a lot of very different people, you don't want to ruin your chances by making such rookie mistakes. After all, Tesla's stock sank by 4% as a consequence of Elon Musk's disrespectful tweet. Who would have thought that he's so emotional...

Writing

Creating social media content is a skill. Not everybody is a writer, let alone an explainer. For some of my coachees, it is very difficult to write about anything—even the subjects they know a lot of.

There are several ways to approach this. If you are really not comfortable with writing, use social media as a notebook. Start with posting links to the articles you've read and found useful—as if you were saving them in your bookmarks. However, even this tiny exercise should bring you out of your comfort zone: make a rule to add your own words to these links, whether it's just a summary of the article or your own opinion on the subject. After all, even if you are just learning something new, the best way to nest the knowledge is to write down the lessons you have learned, rather than only keeping them in mind.

This creates another barrier for many people: they feel embarrassed to post and write about basic things that everybody—or so they think—already knows. This is a false assumption. There are millions of people like you with the same level of understanding. You will do them a favor by explaining something you've learned, in your own words. The truth is that everybody has their audience.

You may not realize it, but even in fiction, the same plot has often been expressed by different authors over and over again—they just use different words and methods of phrasing. The same goes for knowledge in any field, e.g. venture investing.

Pretty much every aspect of this investing practice has been explained on the web multiple times—I've looked it up, trust me. Some of the subjects are easy to explain, and more people read about them and share the best articles many times. However, there are a lot of other subjects that are truly confusing in their explanations. If you search for "Power law in venture capital" or "The Babe Ruth effect in venture capital", you'll be surprised at how very few links you'll find and how poorly they've been shared and liked. The reason for this is because these concepts may be hard to comprehend. Plus, as we've already discussed, venture capital is a very fluid industry—things are constantly changing. Even if there were an article that perfectly explained a subject a year ago, to the extent that no other explanation would ever be needed, the chances that the subject has changed since then, or that new events have affected it, are high, so the explanation would need to be updated and extended.

To sum this up... **never think that you have nothing to say or share with others**.

Along with that, keep in mind that your digital footprint represents a significant part of the foundation of your industry presence, on which you will be building your venture capital career daily thereafter. As soon as you put it out there, it makes you accountable for your choices and reminds you to do your best every day.

Your proficiency in this or that matter will grow over time, and you may one day laugh when reading your very first posts. However, don't be shy of them! Even if you have a different opinion now, or can explain something better than you did before, your older posts only show your consistency and learning curve. After all, you never know whether a person you need to connect with will be satisfied with your LinkedIn profile, or will keep scrolling through your blog to the very first post, and which of your activities will sell you as a person and professional.

It's totally normal, and even advisable, to display your new skills and knowledge on social media as soon as you acquire them. It is okay to point out your own mistakes and even showcase how much your opinion about something has changed over the years, by quoting your old posts and comparing them to where you currently stand. It shows that you are a human, that you have probably made mistakes which you have learned how not to repeat, and this might be a very precious lesson for someone else. It may also be an attractive feature for your potential employer, because as you remember... failures don't matter.

Be thoughtful about your digital footprint, but never be ashamed of your genuine attempts.

Networking

One of the best things an entrepreneur can do is to "get out of the building" and talk to people about his or her product, gathering general opinions and feedback from those who have used it. Getting out of the building is as important for aspiring VCs, however, it doesn't necessarily have to happen offline—the internet helps us save tons of time on this, by allowing us to do a great deal of networking online—sometimes even in a more efficient manner.

Networking is a never-ending topic that requires very basic social skills, without which most careers might stagnate. So, let me only focus on a couple of matters that are most relevant to the job search in venture capital.

First and foremost, networking should never be about yourself. Reaching out to people for the first time and asking for something, is one of the best ways of not getting it.

Networking should be always about the people you want to connect with. This is psychology 101—understanding other people's interests and worries, but instead we more often than not forget about them. This principle is, in fact, one of the foundations of venture investing, because it is all about value creation, which I have mentioned several times already. Entrepreneurs choose investors based on the significance of the value they can create—not just the size of the check. Venture capital firms are also looking for valuable additions to their teams to make them stronger, more diverse, and more attractive to entrepreneurs and limited partners.

Let me give you a couple of examples of tiny things that you can do to connect with your potential employers among VC companies or startups, which can result in a significant advantage when they have to choose between you and another candidate to hire.

1. You can be a promoter of another person by quoting them on social media (don't forget to always tag them).
2. You can assist another person by transcribing what they have said at an event that is open to the general public, and sharing it with others (because they may not have had time to write their thoughts down).
3. Even when you are sending your resume in for an open position, start your email or cover letter with information that may be valuable to the firm (we'll be talking about this in detail in the next section).

Be creative and look for all possible ways to deliver value. Over time, it will all add up and give you exponential results.

There is, of course, a caveat to keep in mind. Because too many people are trying to connect and network with venture investors, with no underlying reason or value, it has become quite annoying. VCs would never admit this, because they prefer to appear as if they are always ready to give advice, but let's keep it real: many of them don't reply to incoming messages, or even read them. So you might want to save your chance until you have something valuable to say. If you do, and get no feedback, it's totally fine—you might still have been noticed, but they (for whatever reason) chose not to announce that fact for now. Be patient—make more bigger bets instead of "spraying and praying".

Events

Among all other possible activities, I often advise to focus on industry events, because they're easy to leverage for the purpose of building your industry presence. There're several ways to approach them.

Firstly, events give you the best networking opportunities concentrated in one place, within a short period of time. You don't need to search for people with certain interests or for potential employers—they are all right there, listed on one page, sometimes even with contact details or at least LinkedIn profiles. As a matter of fact, I am personally not good with business cards, so I save the events brochures instead, with all the speakers listed, for whenever I need to connect with someone.

Secondly, events accumulate a lot of information in a certain field, which you can use to create your own content. Learn, summarize, write it down—it is most likely educational for you and your audience. One of my coachees uses events as straightforward education: "I'm learning whatever I can at the event, and then I search the web for some things that weren't explained clearly enough by the event speakers. After I find answers to all my questions, it feels like I've just completed another online course, but for free."

The beauty of these events, is that you don't necessarily need to physically attend them—again, we have the Internet for that. Many events are being translated online nowadays or become available as recordings after they end. The truth is that even though this is convenient for people who would like to attend the event, but are too lazy to do so, it's not enough. Many of these people wouldn't even have time to watch the events online. This is where an opportunity is created—help them learn from you.

Aside from the video format, you should know how to use other media. For example, attendees and reporters live tweet about the events or write blog posts and articles about what they've heard. You can always use sources like this to find the essence of what's been said, and then make your own summaries and top lists of the entire event. Just imagine what a great opportunity it would be to review an event happening in another country, for your audience that can't travel abroad for the event!

As you can see, this is where things get truly creative and fun.

An unexpected angle to consider, is to become a speaker at an event or a judge for startup competitions. It's natural to think that only famous venture investors get invited to speak at the events. This is not the case at all. Of course, there are high-profile events which not everybody can even attend, but there are others that may be looking for people like you. By that, I mean people who have certain knowledge, regardless of the title on their business card. As long as an event exists, there must be an audience, and this audience may be yours. What value can you provide? Keep reading.

Advising

Don't think that if you are only fit for the most junior position at a VC fund, you have nothing to share with other people. You most definitely have some knowledge that can be of great value to others—whether they are aspiring investors like you or entrepreneurs. You just need to find your superpower.

Anything that can help a startup grow, can be your superpower. Do you have a million subscribers to your album of recipes on Pinterest? Great—share your "secret sauce" about how to grow a fan base with startups who need that kind of information. In fact, many people do that in online courses and earn good money, but they are not planning to work in venture capital, so they aren't really your direct competitors. Focusing on the growth of Pinterest followers for tech startups may be a niche—you just need to recognize it.

You can't predict how attention to detail might play out. For example, Jess Lee, now a partner at Sequoia Capital, planted her future success by writing a cold email to Polyvore (at that time a not very popular online platform), a fashion website that allows users to create shareable collages of clothing and interior designs. She worked as a product manager at Google and just liked spending her free time playing around the website with everything she loved: objects of art, technology, and fashion.

One day, she sent the founder of Polyvore an email with unsolicited, extensive feedback about the website. The email was pretty blunt, instructing the addressee on what she would want: "loading images in search results is slow", "I want image rotation", "Could you add a lightweight way of bookmarking items for future use", and "'Fgnd' and 'Bgnd' are confusing... 'Send to Front' or 'Send to Back' would be more user-friendly".

The founder of Polyvore was so impressed by her advice, that he invited Jess for a coffee, and at the end of that day, offered her a job at Polyvore. Jess joined the company, and after a couple of years, its founding team decided to start recognizing her as an official co-founder of Polyvore due to the significance of her contribution. She then became the CEO of the company and eventually sold it to Yahoo! for ~$200 million in 2015.

Around the same time, the Silicon Valley community was shocked when Michael Moritz, who you are already familiar with, said: "We'll hire women, we just don't want to lower our standards". Since then, it's become fashionable among VC firms to hire women, and a year later, Sequoia Capital hired Jess Lee as the very first female investment partner in the firm's 44-year history. In Sequoia's books, her success qualified her for the high standards of one of the most successful VC firms.

Being hired by a startup is one of the ways of becoming a venture investor. You may not necessarily repeat the path of Jess Lee, but you will still obtain the entrepreneurial experience that venture investors appreciate so much. Whether you have just one piece of advice, or can support a startup as an advisor for some time, this is one of the doors to venture capital—don't miss it!

As I said previously, you may already know all of these approaches and tools that are instrumental for building your industry presence, but knowing them is not enough to actually benefit from them. Finding your place in the system and creating your unique profile in the industry requires a lot of time. If you are currently employed or are studying, it may be overwhelming. Therefore, it is important to structure all of the necessary activities, and optimize the resources you will have to spend on them. I help my coachees create an actionable plan depending on their current skill set and comfort zone. We take them as a baseline and then challenge the status quo by adding new skills and activities over time. On my website, you will find a template for such an actionable plan, among other supplements to this book, so that you can work on this yourself.

In the introduction to this book, I mentioned that to make the tools work, you'll need to practice them and make them habits. Developing any new habit takes time, and some of the activities listed above are no exception. The good thing is that they might not only help you land a job in venture capital in the short-term, but they will remain with you for a long time after that and keep working in your favor.

Don't Spray, Don't Pray (When Looking For A Job)

If you have followed the advice of this book and implemented the suggested techniques, you should have a foundation that you can be confident about. You are, therefore, well enough prepared to apply for a job in venture capital. So, how do you do that?

Well, you don't. Or should I rather say... don't bet on it.

It's a well-known fact that cold applications in venture capital work very poorly. Before I wrote this book, and during my mentorship and coaching program, we tried various strategies to confirm or deny this assumption. It has been confirmed. Even for analyst positions, regardless of how well a candidate matches the job description, replies from hiring VC firms are very rare.

Warm introductions, on the other hand, work only when a candidate can actually be recommended—read: has brought some value to the person who could recommend the candidate. This means that not every venture investor who you are connected to on LinkedIn would want to vouch for you. If you want to rely on warm introductions, then you truly need to have a prior relationship with the person whom you are asking for a recommendation.

An important thing to remember, is that it's not only VC partners whose recommendations count. I have worked with candidates who were referred by associates and entrepreneurs, and got hired.

Therefore, it is really important to work with different audiences and to try and deliver value to all of them.

Another strategy that shows good results, is to reach out to one of the partners or principals directly with an email describing why he or she should consider your candidacy. With this approach you can be truly creative.

This is a well-known tactic when such an email is built on pitching a startup that the fund may be interested in. Another way to make a person read your email is to point at one or two of their portfolio companies, and to explain how you could be helpful to them to boost their growth and achieve exponential returns for the fund. Many venture capital funds are now trying to build platforms to support their portfolio companies—they hire experts in growth, sales, marketing, or other areas, to oversee how each portfolio company performs and direct them if anyone is falling through.

Do your research on each VC firm you are planning to send your resume to, and find something that matches your skill set and investor profile. Don't be afraid to be creative by looking a couple of steps ahead and offering something that is not explicitly said about a fund. For example, one of my coachees pitched his candidacy to a VC firm investing in smart living and housing. The candidate pitched his passion for blockchain technology, showcasing how it can be implemented in this particular sector. The candidate made it to the short list after two interview rounds, and voluntarily dropped out because the firm wanted to hire him in another US state, to where he wasn't ready to move.

Not all VCs publish their job openings in social media—some prefer to look for candidates inside their networks. This is where your work with people from other audiences will count! VCs will be asking their junior staff, portfolio companies, fellow VCs from other funds, and other partnering organizations (like universities, or communities). You see where I'm going with this?

You may also employ a proactive strategy and introduce yourself to a VC firm before they start looking for a new hire. However, it's important to find the right timing for this. For example, when a venture fund is raising or announcing a new fund, it means that the firm will get new funding and they may need to grow the team. Or when a fund makes a new investment and your expertise can help this company grow. If you reach out to a partner with such an offer, it will at least show a few things: you are following the news, you are familiar with their investment focus, and you pay attention to details. At best, you will be hired—for a position at the fund or the new portfolio company. Whatever keeps you close to the job of your dreams, stick to it!

Don't forget that VC funds often hire entrepreneurs-in-residence (EIR). Although it's in the name, there is no written rule that a candidate must necessarily be an entrepreneur. Again, you may have superpowers without being a founder. One of my coachees built his way into VC exactly through the EIR position. He emailed a partner of a fund three times, each time offering his help to three different portfolio companies. He spent a good deal of time learning about those companies and knew exactly what they were doing in the market. After the third email, several weeks later, the partner replied and my coachee got a job as an EIR. At this point, it's just a matter of hard work for him to get hired as an associate or principal, or to move on to another fund.

Whatever tactics you choose, if there is one thing you should not do, it's "spraying and praying". Doing that will only make you look desperate (yes, the candidates' names sometimes circulate between VC firms), and sending your resume with cold emails, or merely applying through LinkedIn or other websites, won't bring you much closer to the goal. You do, however, need to follow a fund's procedures and apply using the suggested links, out of respect for said procedures. If you were not introduced by someone else, a formal application should be followed by a personal email to one of the partners or principals where you mention that you: "applied through the suggested application form, but would also like to introduce myself personally and here is why..."—followed by a description of the value you offer.

If you look at all of these ways to approach a job search from a bird's view, you will see two major frameworks to follow. You will see a system: there will be elements and interconnections between them, some of which you build, other existing connections you might affect, and some of them might affect you. Another discovery is that the process of searching for jobs in venture capital may be constant and therefore, smooth: you are not aggressively looking for a source of income, but are rather open to an opportunity that best matches your investor profile. I like this mature approach the most.

Raise A Fund Yourself

Skipping all of the previously described steps and immediately becoming a general partner in a venture firm, may seem unachievable, however it is not that uncommon. There is even a special term for first-time fund managers—"emerging managers".

Emerging managers have traditionally been identified by their short (or non-existent) investment track records and modest assets under management amounts. The size of "modest" in this context can be determined by a limited partner and differs from one institutional investor to another. Recently, however, the definition of an "emerging manager" was extended and now also relates to female fund managers, managers representing minority groups, and also to those who pursue investment strategies targeting underserved communities or emerging geographic areas. Their background status was also clarified as "having managed fewer than two prior institutional funds" or none.

Raising a venture fund is very similar to raising money for a startup: you need to define your investment thesis (product and market), design your fund's structure and terms (business-model), and sell (pitch) it correctly to the right limited partners (investors).

Limited partners can be divided into two major categories: those who invest in emerging managers and those who don't. The second category takes a very firm position, and it is unlikely that they will invest in you, even if you've built an investment portfolio as an angel investor. For such institutional investors, previous experience managing a venture fund is a must-have for a general partner they'd consider backing.

Those potential limited partners who would gladly invest in emerging managers are wealthy individuals or family offices, but also institutional investors who are dedicated to investing in emerging managers. They have special programs for screening the candidates and "seeding" them. Indeed, they play the same role as seed venture investors, providing capital at a very early stage to help "figure it out".

To sum this up: There is a strong possibility that you will be able to raise your own fund without prior fund management experience, but it will definitely require a lot—and I do mean a lot—of work, but that's what we are here for, right?

There are many things to consider if you decide to raise a venture fund. Even though you can hire lawyers and accountants, you will still need to know all the terms, different alternatives, and specifically, the best practices of fund formation and fund management. Can you ask your attorneys and accountants all the questions that you have? Yes, you can, but they charge per hour and teaching you is not exactly their job. Instead, you can learn about raising a venture capital fund from such resources as the Venture Capital Executive Program (www.vc.academy) and, based on this knowledge, ask them difficult questions relevant to your venture fund in particular. After all, legal and accounting professionals tend to treat knowledgeable clients with more respect and lower bills.

What are the major challenges of the fundraising process?

Above all else, you need to come up with an investment philosophy for your fund, or in venture capital speak—an investment thesis. This includes the determination of:

- The industry, its sectors, and verticals
- The geography
- The size of the investment
- The stage of the companies involved
- Other characteristics of the companies you are going to invest in

Let's say you want to invest in early-stage business-to-customers online services in the United States, for example. The odds that there are hundreds of other venture firms raising money for, or already investing in, the same sector, are very high. Therefore, you will need your differentiator to stand out from competitors when pitching to your potential investors (limited partners). Ultimately, what you're selling to limited partners is your service for growing their wealth. You have a lot of competitors, not only among other venture firms similar or different to yours, but also among other types of alternative investments and asset classes. Therefore, you'd better be sure that your service has a unique offering.

Other things that limited partners worry about are:

- **Your team.** Limited partners don't necessarily need to like you personally (although this helps tremendously, of course), but they need to believe in your team. Building a strong team with the right role distribution is an art.

- **The dealflow.** How will you source potential investments? Will you have early access to deals, etc.? Deals are what you run your business on, which is why they are critical.
- **The investment terms.** Although most funds work according to a traditional business model, it's not set in stone. Its elements can be negotiated if your offer is strong enough.
- **The fund's architecture.** Aligning the operations of a venture firm with its strategy and making them flow smoothly is important. You wouldn't invest in a startup if you didn't believe in their ability to manage a business, so neither would your limited partners.

I can go on and on about raising a fund, starting from the fund formation process, to reporting to the limited partners, and the liquidation of the fund, but for the purpose of this article, let me simplify things. A venture fund is a business just like any other. A general partner in a venture capital firm carries all of the responsibility the same way a startup founder does. If you have never been an entrepreneur yourself, then running a venture fund as a business will be extremely hard for you.

Is it still possible? Practically, yes—if you build your team right. Whether you are looking to be hired or to raise your own fund, you need to become a desired candidate for your potential employer or investor. If you lack something as a general partner, make sure you have other general partners who can fill in the gaps, so that together, you are a dream team.

Why VCs Become Entrepreneurs

Becoming a professional venture investor is a long process. By now, you must surely understand why it takes years. In fact, it may take a couple of years just to find a job in venture capital. Because I show you the different systems of venture capital practice, I cannot ignore a rarely spoken of situation when venture investors... quit.

There may be dozens of reasons why this might happen, starting with an unsuccessful first fund, all the way to being fired for negligence or even improper behavior (you have probably heard about many VC partners who lost their jobs due to alleged sexual misconduct and harassment of female employees and entrepreneurs). However, you can find such cases in many other professions too. A voluntary departure from venture capital in order to become an entrepreneur, is what we are talking about. Why do some venture investors decide to stop investing, to become founders or work for a startup?

Some investors who have done this, had had no entrepreneurial experience before they became VCs at all, so their cases are even more interesting: they chose to become first-time founders with all the accompanying hustle! To make sure I understood their motivation correctly, I interviewed some of the "VCs turned entrepreneurs" about what had caused them to make such an uncommon shift.

The entrepreneurial itch is at all times the main driver when leaving a well-paid job as an investor. The hunger to create and the thirst to scale are both typical for seasoned entrepreneurs. One cannot be an "ex" entrepreneur if it is a true calling. Having entered this river once, you will feel the need to create and grow your own business again and again. On the other hand, observing a business growing rapidly from the front seat is contagious too. Since venture investors are very much exposed to that excitement, it's no wonder that they start feeling the urge to create something—to scale, even if they haven't had entrepreneurial experience before.

"VCs develop a great nose for identifying new opportunities, and at some point in time, the brave ones get the itch to build themselves."
Rohini Chakravarthy, a former partner at private equity (PE) firm New Enterprise Associates (NEA) in the U.S.

Identifying opportunities is a VC's daily job. It's not surprising that when they discover an opportunity they are passionate about, they may wish to start their own business. This is exactly what happened to Rohini Chakravarthy who worked at NEA's (New Enterprise Associates) office in Menlo Park, California for 7 years, and was a partner before she moved back to India to co-found Inksedge—a startup trying to disrupt the event communication space with customized event stationery.

This is also what happened to Paige Craig, who became an investor after shutting down his startup, only to become a vice president of an electric scooter sharing company early in 2018, thereby officially postponing his investing activities. Although he said that the main reason for doing so, was the too high valuations of early-stage companies (and he would like to wait until the market cools down), the startup he joined has become a unicorn itself within only 18 months! This is an unprecedented speed of valuation growth in venture capital practice.

There is no shame is dropping venture investing and becoming an entrepreneur—like I said before, VCs and entrepreneurs are equal.

We've talked about how entrepreneurial experience helps one to become a better VC. But does an investor's experience help one to be a better entrepreneur? Yes—a lot.

The first advantage of changing from being a venture investor to an entrepreneur, is that you will have seen the genesis of hundreds of businesses from the VC perspective. It is a unique opportunity to learn from others' mistakes, by watching their every step, and that gives one a huge leg-up for execution.

The second advantage of having been a VC, is access to a wide network of investors, experts, and strategic partners, each of whom can be crucial to one's business success.

Being a VC also causes you to think in systems, develop critical thinking, and of course, make bigger bets. Seeing markets from a bird's view and finding elements that can affect them, is a stepping stone to a rare ability to predict technology and consumer trends for years, if not decades, in advance—what top tier VCs are known for. Making more big bets and achieving exponential growth as an entrepreneur—this is what any investor would dream of seeing in a portfolio company.

There is of course the opposite opinion:

"Once you work in venture capital, it gets more difficult to become an entrepreneur—you can't beat the lifestyle, and you can bet on companies without taking nearly as much risk as startup founders"
An anonymous investment banker who broke into venture capital

Though investing experience can help you raise money and avoid the common mistakes that many first-time entrepreneurs make, it still doesn't guarantee success for a former VC. Venture investors can be great advisors or even coaches, but they don't do a founder's job every day. What really matters in business, is execution, which implies quite a different role and approach than the typical role of a VC. Changing from an entrepreneur to a venture investor may provide much smoother and more promising career decisions than changing in the opposite direction. However, aside from all the passion of building a great company yourself, there may be other reasons why investors leave their offices on Sand Hill Road.

Being a venture capitalist is not an easy job. It is pretty stressful and provides no immediate rewards. The operational achievements of your portfolio companies aren't your achievements—you can celebrate them, but you don't really feel the success at your fingertips. That is why it may be even more emotionally intense than being a founder. To be completely honest with my readers, I also want to share with you the downsides of being a venture investor.

The Downsides Of Being A VC

Following my promise to challenge your decision to pursue a venture capital career, this whole section is dedicated to the negatives of being a venture investor. I've collected my own experiences, as well as some of what other VCs have dared to say in public.

You may get bored in venture capital

As mentioned a page earlier, one possible reason why some venture investors choose to become entrepreneurs again, or even become first-time founders, instead of continuing their VC paths, is that close proximity to entrepreneurs doesn't satisfy an entrepreneurial itch that they may have. As Andrew Parker, a VC in Palo Alto with Spark Capital, put it: "I don't MAKE anything. Jerry Colonna said it best: Entrepreneurs are pie bakers and VCs are pie slicers. I miss baking sometimes."

If you were an entrepreneur and loved it, you will miss it immensely. If you don't keep yourself busy raising one fund after another, and helping your portfolio companies daily, you will get bored one day, and may decide to quit. There are enough cases where VCs became entrepreneurs, as proof of this, and that is totally fine!

You will be able to leverage all the knowledge and connections you received as an investor, but obviously that is only if you have the luxury of choice and can change your career 180 degrees. If not, then just be prepared to keep yourself occupied so that you don't get disappointed by the lack of entrepreneurial challenges at a VC office.

I know venture investors who are very much into skydiving, racing, or other risky hobbies that help them release their need for adrenaline rushes.

Not many career options for you after venture investing

Everybody (me included) keeps saying that venture capital is a long-term game. Counterintuitively for a "normal" person and typical for a venture investor, it is important to think about your possible exit from a venture capital career upfront (similar to thinking about exits from companies not yet in your portfolio—see the pattern?). The truth is that if you stick with venture capital investing for long, you will lose your hireability—firstly, because you will lose your operational skills as an entrepreneur or manager, and secondly, because having worked at the top of the chain, it'll be pretty hard for you to find a suitable position of a similar rank. Also, if you have lost some of your competencies due to the reasons described above, that will affect the odds as well.

Rob Go, Co-Founder and Partner at NextView Ventures, explained it this way: "It's a lot of fun for a couple years. But after two years, even if you were an operator before, your skills become stale and you are realistically not going to be as good at your former craft as you were before joining venture. Your hireability is still pretty high at that point, but in years 4-6, you start running out of options."

Odds are against you

If you think that you will become a successful venture investor and stay in the industry for decades, remember that nine out of ten startups fail. Now, do a reality check and apply this rationale to your own portfolio.

A partner of a VC firm with three and more partners makes about 2-3 investments per year, while junior partners, principals and associates are on an even slower pace. Each partner of Sequoia Capital tended to make only one (!) investment per any given year. So, you do the math: how many years will you need to work in order to build a meaningful portfolio as an investment team member? While you're worrying about it, the general partners of your firm (and other VC firms) are observing you, to make their decisions regarding your promotion. So effectively, your career depends on a couple of your first investments at a fund which are likely at a stage that is "too early to tell if any of them is a winner".

In a world where most startup companies fail and only about 10%-20% drive a somewhat material return to the fund, the odds of becoming lucky in your early years as a VC, are tough.

Loneliness in venture capital

Despite plenty of networking and partnering with different market players, venture investing is often characterized as a somewhat lonely job. As with many other things in venture capital, this is not a rule, however, and the reality may differ from firm to firm. Comparing a VC firm's office to any startup or corporation, it will more often than not be deserted.

Venture investing is an out-of-office job: partners may travel a lot, attending boards or helping portfolio companies at their offices;

associates spend a lot of time at events and meetings with startups at coffee shops; analysts and other functional staff are busy with their working routine. Of course, partners have weekly meetings and many entrepreneurs come to their offices to pitch, but other than that, most of the job is done by individuals behind closed doors.

Many of my colleagues disagree with this notion, however, and will readily tell you how they foster their corporate culture, which only proves the point. To put it simply, in startups or corporations, teammates spend a lot of time together working on processes towards a common goal, where the VC routine is different, and is best described as a symbiosis of independent units. It's fair to say though, that introverts would appreciate this job. However, they should be that kind of introverts who wear an extrovert hat more often than not.

Venture investing is a negative profession

At this point, you should have felt it. LOL. On a serious note, venture investors say "no" far more often than "yes": out of up to 100 companies that one VC reviews per year, on average, only about one or two get funded. Venture investors reject requests for advice or simply ignore inbound messages far more frequently than they respond to cold emails. You need to learn to say "no", even when you really like an entrepreneur who's pitching you, but their company doesn't match your investment strategy, or they are not a good fit from the venture capital economics standpoint. When you are assessing companies, there is still the calculation of risks and negative outcomes present, so you can't entirely protect yourself from this. Finally, when you advise portfolio companies, it happens more often when things go wrong.

You can, of course, balance this negativity by advising companies that are not part of your portfolio, and educating entrepreneurs by blogging and other proactive measures, however this requires some additional effort, while the negativity keeps chasing you anyway.

VCs are not superheroes

If all that wasn't enough, here is the last downside of being a professional venture capitalist: you are not the superhero that most people think you are. You are not a Robin Hood, nor are you a Superman, and you are not even a knight in shining armor—no matter how much you desire to be a supportive advisor to entrepreneurs, you are a cold-blooded money manager before everything else. Deal with it.

Venture capitalists put a lot of effort into harvesting their image as a "founder's best friend", because if you cut to the chase, our profession is only slightly different from that of the wolves of Wall Street. Venture investors also buy low and sell high, and each deal for us, is a financial transaction bound by strict legal terms. Once it's signed, we are truly entrepreneurs' best friends. I'm being overly sarcastic of course, but this is the hard truth.

Professional venture investors invest with the ultimate goal of making big returns. Everything else is secondary.

We have discussed that venture capitalists manage the money of limited partners, and are therefore liable for such returns. As such, they cannot invest in companies that they don't believe are the right fit, even if they like the founders a lot. Angel investors don't do charity either—if returns don't matter much to you, then there is a multibillion dollar world of philanthropy at your disposal. Even impact investors, who may seem to care more about impact than financial returns, are on a mission to prove that impact investing provides market returns that are no worse than traditional venture capital investing. So there you have it—it's all about a pay-off.

We have talked about money as being one of the main motivators of venture investors, so this negative aspect shouldn't create an issue. However, you should make it clear to yourself and the entrepreneurs you work with, that you are their business partner and not their friend, even though you are willing to share their mission to change the world. **You don't make emotional decisions, you do the job of multiplying your limited partners' wealth to the best of your abilities.**

I'd like to finish this "negative" section on a positive note, however. There are thousands of venture investors around the world, and they deal with these downsides on a daily basis. Some, of course, drop out with disappointment, and this is exactly why I always point out the possible downsides of the profession, in order to make you aware of them and to arm you with the tools and solutions you would need to stay satisfied with your career choice.

The Industry Needs A New Generation Of Investors

This is the last section of this book, and here I want to explain why the venture capital industry needs a new generation of investors, and why I try to find such. By now, you may have gotten the impression that the venture capital industry works as efficiently and reliably as a Swiss watch, but if you look at it as a system, you'll see the flaws.

Venture investing brought to light a lot of true innovations. However, venture capital itself is one of the most conservative industries, which, in fact, hasn't changed much throughout the decades, and still uses a business model from the year 1800.

The "two and twenty" model, according to which fund managers get 2% of the fund's size annually as a management fee, and 20% of the profit of the fund as "carry" or "carried interest", was first implemented in whaling in the XIX century—a hunt for whales to use their oil as a fuel. Captains of such expeditions would assemble teams and raised money from many investors, as this was quite an expensive and risky venture. The investors couldn't question the captain's decisions, and covered all of the ongoing costs, such as food and supplies for the crew by paying 2% of the total funds raised. If an expedition was successful, at the end of a voyage, the team would get 20% of the whale meat (carry), with investors retaining the other 80%. Although the actual percentages may vary today, the model has not changed, and this arguably harms the entire industry.

Many venture investors would admit to that in private conversations, but the existing inertia keeps them from changing the model—"If it ain't broke, don't fix it". Some venture investors are very vocal about the problems created by this model, but there are too few of them to bring a change to the entire industry. Hence, venture capital still stands on the "two and twenty" structure, because that's how things have always been done.

So what is wrong with venture capital?

The major weakness of the "two and twenty" model is that the annual management fee is the main incentive for venture investors. Most VCs never see carry, and even if they do, it may turn out to be only a fraction of what they received from the management fee over the lifecycle of the fund. The management fee is paid regardless of whether the portfolio companies succeed, so there is a clear incentive to build larger funds, because 2% annually of a $1 billion fund is exactly four times more than that of a $250 million fund for the same amount of work. Shouldn't larger funds have more investments, and therefore, more work to do?

According to a 2013 World Economic Forum report, it takes the same amount of time to conduct due diligence on a $10 million investment as it does on a $100 million investment. Therefore, if a fund prefers making a few larger deals rather than many smaller deals, there is no obvious reason for the management team to get a four times bigger management fee. Especially when considering the fact that a larger fund will require bigger exits to return it, so this management team will likely be reluctant to risk investing in breakthrough innovations, and keep picking the startups that resemble what has worked in the past.

Once they see a pattern, they prefer investing in larger deals that are easier to understand, than in several smaller deals that don't fit a familiar pattern. This is when the canonic "two and twenty" model really hurts the world, and is the reason why, at some point in history, Silicon Valley started investing more money in meaningless mobile applications than in life-changing innovations.

Investing based on patterns for the sake of returning larger funds is a pure evil in venture capital, which is supposed to fuel risky innovations, by definition. With patterns comes investing in white founders, instead of diversifying through ethnicities. Patterns make venture investors pour most of their funds mainly into only two regions of the United States—Northern and Southern California on the West Coast, and New York and Boston on the East Coast. Finally, it's pattern investing that makes female founders struggle for venture dollars, because VCs are more comfortable investing in men.

Mega-funds of the size of a billion dollars or more are somewhat new in the market that only became a trend last year. While Silicon Valley venture firms were competing with each other to raise funds of around $1 billion, Softbank's went all-in and announced a $100 billion fund in 2017. Not only did it leave "ordinary" single billion dollar funds that couldn't possibly compete behind, but it, of course, greatly affected mere multi-hundred-million-dollar firms.

More money in the market led to many companies being overvalued in the Series A rounds. The valuations are now determined by how much investors are willing to pay—and not by reasonable business metrics. In the current highly competitive venture capital market, smaller investors have to agree to these terms. They try to justify the higher ticket price with the power law, but blindly copying playbooks of larger and more experienced firms doesn't necessarily work for smaller venture investors, and nothing guarantees them sufficient returns.

More than $1 trillion in committed capital in private equity and venture capital funds worldwide doesn't mean that smaller funds will be failing. They will have to, however, create their own, new playbooks, because all of those that were previously used to invest with, are by now out of their league. In this very unbalanced situation in venture capital, and the newly created crypto investing market, where a lot of the smart people and smart money is going, nothing is certain.

Just think about that: blockchain and cryptocurrencies stormed into the venture capital industry! Token sales raised only ~$95 million in 2016, but almost $3.7 *billion* in 2017. More than $16.5 *billion* has already been raised in 2018, even though we are only halfway through the year. How could nobody have seen this coming? Even Andreessen Horowitz, a venture capital firm which has always been regarded as avant-garde, is only creating a purely crypto dedicated fund now.

"...So times they are a changing in VC land right now. Which mirrors the broader tech sector which is maturing and consolidating while a next wave starts brewing. How to play this whole thing is challenging. The future of the VC business and its top firms are in flux and those who play it right stand to gain a lot and those who don't stand to lose a lot. It is most definitely not a time for the status quo."
Fred Wilson, co-founding partner at Union Square Ventures

Those venture investors who have stayed in their comfort zone and played by the old rules, will have to join those very few investors who had been ready for a change long ago. It's really hard to change your game after playing it the same way for decades, so the younger VCs, who haven't yet planted their roots in old-school venture capital, have better odds of making it.

Back in 2012, Bill Gurley, a partner at Benchmark, said: "Youth is a competitive weapon. Young VCs are open to new ways of doing things. This form of "rule-breaking", or intentionally ignoring yesterday's doctrine, may in fact be a requirement for successful venture capital investing." If only people had listened to him back then and started changing the venture capital model, we would probably be more prepared for the changes that are happening today.

On the upside, we are now at the point where new rules of venture investing are being created and tested, and you personally can join the movement. It'll take some time to turn the ship in a different direction: almost all of the current venture firms will have to return the billions to limited partners first—so you still have time to learn. Some of you will sooner rather than later join venture firms that are currently playing by the old rules. Others will start creating something entirely new. Both instances are the reasons why I have been working on democratizing the knowledge of venture investing—so that you can affect its future. I've been collecting the knowledge base for venture capital, to show how it has been working so far, and what needs to (and can) be changed. I also wrote this book, not to give you false promises, but to inspire you and to help the industry breed a new generation of venture investors. I believe we are now one step closer to this goal!

Good luck!

ASSIGNMENT 5

The final product of the coaching program is an action plan that includes both specific to-do's to create your industry presence, and finding a job in venture capital. Although the worksheet I have created for this is pretty comprehensive, there is lot of room for creativity!

You don't need to do EVERYTHING that is suggested by the worksheet, however, it is critically important that you will not stay in your comfort zone, and that you will keep adding must-do's to your action routine.

RESOURCES

www.renata.vc

www.vc.academy

Made in the USA
Las Vegas, NV
20 July 2021